LIFE IN THE CONTINUUM

Explorations into Human Existence,
Consciousness & Vibratory Evolution

LIFE IN THE CONTINUUM

Explorations into Human Existence,
Consciousness & Vibratory Evolution

KINGSLEY L. DENNIS

THE ABE COMMENTARIES, VOL. I

THE WAY BACK HOME SERIES

BEAUTIFUL TRAITOR BOOKS

Other books by Kingsley L. Dennis

UNIFIED: Cosmos, Life, Purpose

*Hijacking Reality: The Reprogramming & Reorganization
of Human Life*

*Healing the Wounded Mind: Mass Psychosis in the Modern World &
The Search for Self*

The Modern Seeker: A Perennial Psychology for Contemporary Times

The Sacred Revival: Magic, Myth & the New Human

*Bardo Times: hyperreality, high-velocity, simulation, automation,
mutation - a hoax?*

*The Phoenix Generation: A New Era of Connection, Compassion and
Consciousness*

*Dawn of the Akashic Age: New Consciousness, Quantum Resonance,
and the Future of the World* (co-authored with Ervin Laszlo)

Breaking the Spell: An Exploration of Human Perception

*New Revolutions for a Small Planet: How the Coming Years Will
Transform Our Lives & Minds*

*The Struggle for Your Mind: Conscious Evolution and the Battle to
Control How We Think*

New Consciousness for a New World

CONTENTS

PREFACE

I n my previous book – *UNIFIED: Cosmos, Life, Purpose – Communicating with the Unified Source Field & How This Can Guide Our Lives* – I presented a body of communications received from the Unified Field by my friend and colleague Nicola Mortimer. I wrote *UNIFIED* to give a scientific and philosophical context to the hypothesis that humanity could be in communication with the source of pure consciousness from which all matter (materiality) and life emerges. In the first part I outlined my reasoning, supported by scientific research, to give credibility to this hypothesis. I presented the messages/communications in the second part of the book. In the third part, I explored some broader philosophic reflections upon what it means to be living within an interconnected field of consciousness energy. Yet at no time did I give a deep dive into the messages themselves; preferring instead to leave them untouched for the reader to make their own speculations and gain their own reflections without author intervention. Then one unsuspecting morning I picked up a copy of *UNIFIED* that was on my shelf and began leafing through some of the messages in part two of the book. Without planning, I started to write down a few words, initially for myself, that I thought would explain – in my own words – some of the meaning being transmitted in the messages. Then I kept on writing more, as it seemed to flow effortlessly. I soon realized that I was gaining more clarity from the Abe material for myself in this way. In re-turning to re-read some of the Abe messages, I felt that there was a depth of knowledge and ideas that deserved greater scrutiny and unpacking. Some unspoken urge within me nudged me to go on. It seemed the right thing to do to give voice to some of my own thoughts and understandings as a way of bringing out more depth of meaning contained in these communications. As I was writing, I sensed that the information given in the Abe communi-cations, as they are called, were very much for these moments we are living through now.

Some of the later communications in this volume discuss the theme of humanity and its future. We are told that humani-ty is now within the period of rethinking its choices. This is the readjustment period, and within this moment there will be some experiences of discomfort. I share a quote from the Abe commu-nications: 'It will be one of discomfort, for all readjustment is uncomfortable. For if you have been sitting in a certain position for a while, when you come to move to another position it is of discomfort, is it not?' This suggests that the degree of discomfort will depend upon how strongly we remain attached to our old patterns and paradigms, or how willing we are to shift to a new pattern-resonance. These are the times we now find ourselves within. For this reason, and more, I feel that it is important to share these commentaries. If anything, the Abe messages have gained in significance – at least for me. I had other 'aha!' moments when writing these commentaries, as if gaining a deeper level of understanding of what these communications are attempting to convey. There are concepts and themes we need to grasp: such as, everything is vibration. Yes, I know it is easy to say this. Certain self-development teachings have been saying this for decades:

but what does it really mean? Or rather, what practicality does it have for us? I hope that these commentaries can bring some clarity to these understandings, and many more.

I do not wish to say too much at this point as the following commentaries should speak for themselves. I should say that these are my interpretations of the Abe communications, and my interpretation alone. I am sharing here what my reading of the material has brought forth from within me. I am not saying that I am right. I am only saying that this is what I intuitively felt from my own readings, and that I wished to share for the reader to make their own reflections. I can only hope that your own reflections will bring some benefit and clarity to your understanding, as they did for me. I'd like to think that we are having a conversation between and with ourselves.

Kingsley L. Dennis
January 2022

NOTES

i) ON THE ABE COMMUNICATIONS

They are a series of Questions and Answers between two people – Nicola and myself – and Abe. The Abe materials are positive and inspiring communications that urge us to find our way back into balance – from a 'splintered mind' into 'home resonance.' These communications are **not** a channeling but an *allowing*. This first volume of communications contains over 200 questions and answers covering such topics as physical and mental health, society, culture, religion, technology, the cosmos, human evolution, any many more. This material has been 'allowed' at this time for it is essential that humanity finds its home resonance and comes back into a harmonious relationship with itself and the world.

Nicola receives the Abe communications in a kind of 'stream of consciousness' style. That is, the words are almost entirely without punctuation and consist of continuous words rather than sentences. After I receive the communications, I read through them and do my best to format them into grammatical sentences. It appears that the sentence style can be somewhat 'archaic' at times. There are many 'but see,' 'but hear this,' 'see this,' and similar phrases. Actually, to be fair, these are very useful markers as they allow me to see where one sentence finishes and another one begins. There were times also when Abe seemed to say something in a way that was not the most fluid, or modern way of expression. I wondered if Abe wanted for me to 'translate' their communications into a more flowing, informal manner. Abe replied: 'If you feel extremely strongly to do so, then yes. We would also like to say that if you are on the borderline of wanting to, then we feel it should be kept as it is.'

There you have it – we were given permission to make alterations only if we felt 'extremely strongly' to do so. Otherwise, we were to leave it alone. Perhaps there was good reason for this. Maybe, just maybe, the transmission style of Abe is also impacting us as we read – acting upon our own inner cognition? The point to repeat here is that these communications are not to be regarded as a form of 'channeling' as is commonly known. Channeling usually takes place between an entity and a human being: often this entity is a discarnate spirit, a sentient intelligence/species, or other form of non-terrestrial being. Yet, in this case, the communications are being received from the Source of Ourselves. In other words, we are in communication with the 'higher,' or non-manifested, part of our soul. For this reason, we were informed not to regard this as a channeling but as an *allowing*. We are 'allowing' a part of our incarnated self to communicate with the Unified Source. We are, so to say, not in contact with another 'being' but with our own Being. And since each person has this ability, this contact, it is regarded as a form of 'allowing' – we only need to *allow* ourselves.

Another point to raise is that in these initial communications – or *allowances* – most of the messages were signed off with 'Love & Light.' This may seem like a cliché in many channeled or 'new age' material. Yet the reason for this became evident in our later series of communications (not in this book) when Abe shifted from 'Love & Light' to 'Allowance & Light.' The energy of 'love' then became the energy of *allowance* that is central to how all forms of consciousness relate. There will be more to say on this switch in later volumes of the Abe material. What I would like to point out here is that we should not take the phrase 'Love & Light' at face value but also recognize for how it represents the various states of existence. Love represents pure consciousness, the Source of All That Is. And Light represents the photons or building blocks of materiality. All matter is created from the density of photonic arrangement; that is, we are essentially light beings. Therefore, by signing off with the phrase 'Love & Light' Abe is in fact, to my mind, signifying the unity of no-form and form: of Pure Consciousness (Love) and of Matter (Light).

ii) ON THE USE OF TERMS: Abe and Continuum

Why are these materials referred to as the 'Abe Communications'? I do not wish to repeat here what was previously said in the *UNIFIED* book regarding the background of how I came into contact with Nicola Mortimer and the Abe messages. However, I would like to address the naming aspect. Nicola Mortimer, who received these communications, wished to have some form of identification. When she expressed this, the name 'Abe' was given. Of course, these communications are with the unified field of pure consciousness and so there is no 'name' here. Yet you know how humans are – we like to know with whom we are having a conversation! Later, in the first session of our Q&A, I addressed this issue of why the moniker of Abe. This is the reply we received:

'this was a fitting name to that of which you would say abbreviation in that we can be of contraction...ABE was short for abbreviation: abbreviation meaning a term that is of something that is of contraction; shortened, lessened...' (S.1.Q33)

What this says is that even by using a name we are dealing with a contraction, an abbreviation, of the original form. A 'name' is a contraction – a 'shortened, lessened' form – of the origin of that which is represented by the name. Thus, a name is an abbreviation; and a further contraction, or abbreviation, of the word 'Abbreviation' is **Abe**.

Later, at the close of the first book of communications, Abe again makes mention of this. They state:

See it as a radio station in which you would like to listen to. You tune in to certain channel, but you see you have but no preference and it is allowing more to come forth. Like we say, ABE is just a shortened constriction, of the whole thing - an abbreviation of pure consciousness. (S.5.Q29)

The name that we use and which we were given – Abe – represents 'an abbreviation of pure consciousness.' For me, that makes sense. I hope it does to the reader too. Abe has never been wholly a 'form.' As a unity, it is formless. Yet it can be expressed through form: 'For whatever is form, we are of it... So, we have never been into form, but our formlessness allows to be in all form but not of it' (S.1.Q34)

Abe is not a being, a person, a species – Abe is *Everything*. Abe is the source of all manifestation: the collective Source Field from which all materiality is birthed. It is also both you and I. Abe refers to itself as the collective Source - yet prefers to use the term Unity. Unification is a major theme of Abe's communications. In the words of Abe:

> We are but your original state of being, it is just that you do so have conditions of a body which creates different vibratory interference in a way. For you see, we do not have a physical body and are not of a point of place only, but when in communication with you both…We want to guide you to the way back home, here and now.

The Continuum of pure consciousness can be within all form whilst not being the form itself. We could say this another way: the Continuum is *in form but not of the form*.

Why have I chosen now to use the term *Continuum*? Again, these are all names; and names are a way for humans to categorize, interpret, and define something. And this is very difficult when it comes to attempting to interpret and represent something that is beyond form. However, using terms such as *Unified Field, Source Field, Zero-Point Field*, also have their associations that may bring some distortion with them. In this instance, I have chosen upon the term *Continuum* (of Latin origin) for, according to various dictionary definitions, a continuum is something that keeps on going, whilst allowing for change slowly over time. It also signifies that the whole is made up of many parts, and this continuous whole has parts that cannot be separated or separately discerned.[1]

....

1   https://www.yourdictionary.com/continuum

What are examples of a continuum? Again, a dictionary definition gives us *frequency* as an example of a continuum, and states further that: 'a continuous series of elements or items that vary by such tiny differences that they do not seem to differ from each other. An example of a continuum is a range of temperatures from freezing to boiling.[2] This 'range of temperatures' also represent the various degrees of energy: from freezing (form) to boiling (no form). A continuum contains all these various states of energy including everything in-between. A continuum is the whole as well as all the degrees of its parts. Furthermore, it is continuous while allowing for degrees of change. In order not to overly make use of pre-determined names, such as *Source Field* or *Zero-Point Field,* I felt that for the benefit of greater understanding we could use a more neutral term: *Continuum.* The only further addition I would make here is to say that the *Continuum* that I refer to is whole, pure consciousness. I hope the reader will allow me this discretion.

iii) REFERENCING

All quotations and citations in the text are taken from the Abe communications (see Part Two). No outside material is referenced. When you see a few words in speech marks 'like this' then they are the words of Abe that I am bringing into my sentences. Longer citations and quotes are referenced according to the section and question/answer from where they are located. For example, when it is written (S.2.Q10), then this refers to Section 2, Question 10. I have gone through the sections, with their questions, in a chronological order from beginning (S.1) to end (S.5).

••••••••••••••••••

2   https://www.yourdictionary.com/continuum

The sections can be found in Part Two of this book, and are in exactly the same order as they appear in the *UNIFIED* book. That is, Section One – Setting the Scene; Section Two – Mind, Body & Spirit; Section Three – Human Society & Culture; Section Four – Science & Technology; and Section Five – Humanity & its Future.

INTRODUCTION

'Once you have touched it there is no division; no tearing your heart away. For it knows no separation.'
Oracle of Apollo from Anatolia

I t is strange, very odd, that humanity has arrived this far along its journey and yet still clings to such antiquated thinking. Even today, vast numbers of people still think that when they die, that's it. They're dead. Gone. No more. Life *after* death of the physical body sounds incredible still for so many. Why should this be? Why do so many people continue to believe that life is a one-off transitory affair? It's a belief of separation. A life of a momentary blip in the vastness of things. It is time to change our thinking, in mass. That is, not just scattered individuals but collectively – as a whole species. We have to relearn – to *re*-member ourselves – in order to recognize that all life is intrinsically connected as all life remains a part of the same energy source. Matter is a state of vibration. Just as water can be liquid, solid, and vapour; so too can frequency be energy fields, waves, and physical particles. Everything in manifestation has come forth through a change in energy frequency. Everything is vibration. The Abe materials say this; the inventor Nikola Tesla said the same thing. Form comes into being from no-form. At all times, form is related and connected to the energy state of no-form.

Human life – in fact, all life – is more than that which our physical eyes can see. Our senses are limited whilst they are contained within a state of physical slumber. That is, we each know – instinctively in our depths – that we are more than the physical vehicle we inhabit. Religions have been attempts at re-binding us to this lost knowledge of our innate existence within the infinite consciousness pool. The word 'religion' comes from the Latin word *religare* – to bind. Through religious practices we are being compelled to remember and recognize (re-cognize) our inherent bond to the Source of which we are a manifestation at the physical energetic component. And yet, within our cultures we are said to be 'spiritual' when we attempt to pursue these paths and practices of remembrance and bonding. However, why should it be deemed 'spiritual' to be pursuing our natural heritage – our lineage of existence? To exist is to be 'spiritual' for we are endlessly upon a path of the spirit, of the soul. We are souls incarnated. We are having a life experience through the vehicle of a physical body. To be alive is to be spiritual for we are that Spirit. Why do we define and categorize the 'spiritual' as being something other, something apart? Why have we been denying ourselves for so long?

In the words of Abe, we have been running around chasing our own tails. As human beings, we have a tendency to get in our own way most of the time. It is time then to step away from ourselves in order to allow the vital flow of life energy to move through us, without the constant blockage. The tangible and intangible co-exist as aspects of the same thing. We are Source energy and matter at the same time: spirit and biology co-existing as a merger. It is time to honour that mergence by healing our fragmentation. We are, as Abe constantly reminds us, splintered minds. We have dropped the phone line and lost sight of the conversation: the

conversation between self and Self. They are one and the same –
a part of and never apart from. It is this understanding that we
now need to embrace if we wish to thrive as a species in physical
embodiment. If we are unable to recognize these fundamental
truths, then we are liable to slip out of alignment with our evolutionary path. And if we are out of resonance with our evolutionary journey then we fall into stagnation – and ultimately, we fail
to evolve any further. We come to the end of our physical line.
Life goes on elsewhere, in other manifestations and expressions.
Life always *is* and will *forever be*. Where shall we be? Where shall
we place ourselves within the grand cosmic tapestry of living
expression?

There *is* a meaning to life. There is a meaning to everything for
existence is *pure meaning*. Whether as part of the formless Source,
or whether as a pinpoint of physical expression, we are meaning-
ful. We are *pure existence*. We are *all that is* and *all that ever will be*.
We are in a dance, a conversation, a relationship, with ourselves.
You, me, everything. The fragmentation we see around us is only
a perceived aspect of the wholeness – not apart from it. It is up to
us to close that gap – to re-join the party.

Wake up world. There is everything before us – if we can open our
eyes and re-bind, or energetically align, with our home resonance.

PART ONE:

THE COMMENTARIES

Remember - the harvest of the seed is in preparation of the food.

ABE

SECTION ONE – Setting the Scene

Communicating with the Unified Field

I n these communications there is a strong emphasis upon the notion of 'allowance.' What this refers to is that the person tends to get in the way of themselves – they are their own blockage. We are each receiving signals and 'nudges' all the time, yet we are unaware of this. We each have the capacity to listen to that *special voice* within us; yet seldom do we listen. Or we do not listen attentively enough. The more we can 'allow ourselves,' we are told, then the more we can play a part in our own development and evolution. As the individual evolves, so too does this assist the collective.

The allowance of these communications is related to our own personal evolvement. The human being, it is said, is like an antenna that picks up radio waves. As a physical individual, we can act as the 'point of place' for the localization of the communication. Yet the communication is available in all times and places for there is no time or space involved in the existence of the Unified Field. As Abe says: 'What is enabling us to come through is that the mind is expanding as you evolve. This will be so, as to let in more and more. What we want to do too is to enable this transition.' (S.1.Q2). As our perceptual ranges expand and

3

open up – or rather, as we move past our conditioning – we are able to receive and/or communicate more with the intelligence fields beyond our reality set. Within the same passage, Abe goes on to state:

> As to what is happening, we feel that at this time there is an epidemic as people are struggling. You see, like we say, you are stagnant, and you cling to this in your form. Energy is shifting you along and coming in to help flow, but like a dog with a bone you will not let go. (S.1.Q2).

Indeed, there is an epidemic currently – physically, psychologically, and spiritually. It is a fair comment to say that many people are 'stagnant' at this time as we are blinded by the state of being in our physical form. We are informed that energy is 'coming in to help flow' and yet humans are blocking this energy as we are clinging to our materialistic perspectives like a dog with a bone, and not being able to drop these in order to 'allow' more receptivity with intangible energies.

As part of our entanglement with materiality we have to deal with the concept of time, and our insistence that we exist as 'solid individuals' within a certain time construct. Time, Abe says, is part of our human structure, and it has been utilized as a means for us to prove 'I am here' because we can time locate ourselves (S.1.Q3). This then creates a time sequence where existence is located and divided into sections. Past time sections are parts of our memory. The future is already in existence; it only has not been actualized into our experience. It is because of this time-location construct – of dividing and segmenting the life experience – that we have difficulty in perceiving the interrelatedness of all things. It is this interrelatedness that is the collective consciousness – a web of consciousness 'through all of time and space and place experience' – that is the Abe (the Continuum) that we all can attune to (S.1.Q4). Everything is an eco-system of interwoven energy levels. There is no separation, only a distinction of levels. The energy of the Continuum exists through all levels for all levels are a manifestation of its existence: cosmic, environmental/planetary, and bodily: 'all different levels, perceptions, points of place working in perfect harmony at each and every level but non-separated at all.' (S.1.Q4) The connection with the Continuum (Unified Field, Brahma, Source, etc) is a knowledge that has always existed and yet humanity has largely lost, or become detached from, this understanding. What we are being urged to do now is to make that reconnection. It is not some fantastical or ridiculous notion; if anything, it is a natural inheritance that has become dormant for the vast majority of humanity. The Abe communications are intended to enable us to see this interconnection: '…this vastness of perceptual experience; that there is a wholeness in this separation and that which looks like discord at one level is harmony at another.' (S.1.Q4)

This is a fundamental point that underlies these communications: that beyond the apparent separation there is a wholeness. Currently, humanity is experiencing this reality as a form of separation; and in this, there is discord and disharmony. Yet, says Abe, there is harmony at another level – at the level of wholeness. Throughout human history, philosophers of all ages and epochs have wrestled with the big questions over the meaning of existence, exploring and critiquing our forms of knowledge. Abe puts it more simply: 'True knowledge from our standpoint is allowing that in which you are.' (S.1.Q4) That is, all knowledge is available through us for we are all that we need to know – *if only* we can allow ourselves to be our true selves. The mystery of knowledge is what we have cloaked ourselves with; in each age we don a new overcoat, until we have arrived at the present time where we are submerged beneath all the layers we have place upon us. We are not able to access the kernel, the seed – our inner truths. Abe says it beautifully in this way: 'All knowledge is knowable, it is just that you think that it has to be attained - every experience, everything, every flap of a wing, crush of a rock, birth of a child, cry of a death, are all a vibration, a part of a pattern intrinsically interwoven into a web of consciousness.' (S.1.Q4) Everything that Abe knows, we can know too. There is no separation or division, other than the ones we have placed upon us (or allowed others to place upon us). The point now is that we need to unravel ourselves before we are able to truly go forward again in a balanced and rightful way. If we keep trying to push ahead, then it will be as if trudging through mud that is knee high. We are not only weighing ourselves down but, more importantly, we are forging ahead with a skewed sense of who we truly are. Furthermore, we may be attempting to create a future for us that is based on faulty thinking, narrowed perceptions, and incomplete understanding of our place within the bigger picture. We are being told now that what we have within us is much more expansive than what we are attaching to ourselves externally. We now have technologies that connect us globally and allow for instantaneous communication and contact. Yet we are more expansive than this within our essence. The life experience has caused humanity to become fixated upon the physical constructs to the detriment of our innate intelligence that connects us to a reservoir of cosmic consciousness. This Source-Consciousness is available to all people; it is this knowledge and understanding that has been lost to us. Primarily, it has been the distraction of the physical that has pulled us away from our innate knowing and contact.

To understand how such communications operate, it is necessary to accept that all life is vibrational. All physical life is in vibrational communication and, in one form or another, in vibrational correlation. Vibrational correlation is another form of energetic inter-relationality. Just because it is not visible to us, does not deny its existence. Many people are becoming more aware of this through published research about how the natural environment communicates between itself: trees to trees; animals to their environment, and more. Life is an interwoven web of communication. As humans, we are overly focused upon the types of communication that are quantifiable – or 'knowable.' This means either through the spoken word, the written word, and other mediums that *show* the communication to us. As a consequence of our attachment to the physical paradigm of reality, we only seem to validate those things which show up for us: 'As so with the whole of life – communication is of essence and with correct knowledge of what that actually means is of essence.' (S.1.Q5) Within correct vibratory correlations, such as within parts of the human body, harmony is necessary and is the essence of correct alignment. Yet harmony is not so much something to be sought and strived for, as in trying hard to reach out to grasp it. Rather, harmony is 'something allowed and opened up to.' The Continuum, likewise, is not above and beyond humanity, for it is an intrinsic part of who we are: '…we are a part of that in which you are and in which everything is. We want to show you this; to be open to the beauty of contraction and expansion.' (S.1.Q5)

This contraction and expansion is a continual dipping in and out of material form. The Continuum is interwoven with all forms of existence and, like our breathing, is coming in and out of form. Abe refers to this as a 'constant becoming.' These constant 'becomings' are recognized as forms of vibrational alignment. We are only able to grasp a part of what this means as we need to

7

evolve our physical mechanisms to receive more of this vibrational alignment. To evolve as a species, we first need to understand that we are much more than our physical bodies – or, as Abe says, our physical point-of-place. We are told that for energy to experience physicality it needs a point of attraction. This 'point of attraction' in our case is the human body – this is our 'mechanism.' The energy that can come through, or align, with the mechanism depends upon the capacity of the mechanism to receive it. There needs to be a correlation. As way of analogy, a strong electrical current from the power station first needs to pass through transformers to step down the power for it to be received at the household point-of-place. If the energy was not first passed through these transformers, then it would blow all the fuses at the other end. There must be a vibrational match for there to be a correlation. As Abe states: 'as you evolve you will too see that the whole cosmos is alive.' (S.1.Q7)

All the cosmos is alive and intertwined. There is no separation at all at the fundamental level. It is only the physical construct, as Abe calls it, that could perceive any separation at all. And within the greater picture, there is life within the cosmos that is evolving at different rates – different modalities of physicality. All life is essentially evolving within the Continuum back to Source state from which it came, and to which it is inseparable. There is expansion and contraction, yet there is nothing outside of this. All life is inclusive and contains itself as well as all there is and all there will ever be.

Abe states that the Unified Field consciousness of the Continuum is there to assist but not to direct. It can be surmised that the Source-of-Self is wishing to assist in the correlation of energies – the communication between and with itself – but not to direct or interfere too strongly with the passage, or life experience, of the various manifestations. Those life experiences that

8

are more constricted to their physical expression will have less receptivity to the flow of subtle energies. It is almost natural for us to consider other forms of conscious expression as *intelligence*. It is a word that many of us use, including myself, to refer to other forms of sentience. It is interesting to note that Abe states that the word *intelligence* has been anthropomorphised or overly personified from the human perspective: 'As for the word intelligence, we would say that it is really been over-humanised for intelligence is the way in which you collaborate and harmonise with your environment. It really is not something to gain but to be relational to.' (S.1.Q8) Intelligence indicates the way of harmonization and collaboration. And importantly, it is not an attribute to be gained but to be in relation to. Here is an early reference to the term *relational*. This concept of relational becomes central to the Abe communications and crops us frequency in all later messages. We shall come back to this later in greater depth as it forms a core understanding of the Abe material. Communication is the act of vibrational alignment. We can say that we are able to communicate with all that we are vibrationally aligned with. We can testify this from common sense. Have you ever tried to communicate with someone who is 'not on your wavelength'? In most cases, we say that there was not a meeting of like-minds. Or that we were unable to see 'eye to eye.' All in all, there is a disjunction that is often described in bodily terms. It is also a psychological situation, for alignment is generally blocked by the layers of our social conditioning. Our point-of-place expression – i.e., our physical body and mindset – has multiple layers of filters that most of the time are not known to us. When a person is entrenched in their personality, they are less likely to be in vibrational alignment with aspects of the non-visible realm, such as with energetic fields of consciousness. Each person is a *vibrational signature*. This signature that is unique to each person is formed from a combination of factors; principally, it is a reflection of our state of openness and degree of conditioning filters. The less filters we have, the more aligned we can become. The more we fall into a natural state, free from our social personality, our socio-cultural beliefs, our opinions, and similar baggage that we have come to associate with our 'self,' then the closer we are to an energetic state of vibrational receptivity.

The expression of consciousness that manifests through each person is aligned with the frequency resonance of the body-mind vehicle (what we would call 'the person'). The receptivity of consciousness is restricted according to the conditioning of the person; these are the filters of the brain and body. The brain especially has many filters as the brain of a person is more susceptible to programming and forms of external conditioning, such as through schooling and propaganda. In other words, it can be said that we 'allow' consciousness to come through us. This process is what has often been referred to as *inspiration*. Yet for many people, inspiration is something regarded as originating from oneself; i.e., from a person's own ideas and thinking. In this way, we refer to people as creatives, geniuses, etc, which only leads to a strengthening of a person's identification with their personality/ego rather than liberation. This may result in the opposite effect, which is further blocking the allowance of consciousness ('inspiration') and a blockage of creativity. In this regard, it is unhelpful to refer to oneself as a genius if you wish to continue to be inspired!

The allowance and receptivity of the unified consciousness field – the Continuum – is related also to the particular pathways that we have within the human brain. As Abe stated: '…we have been able to come through previously and this is because of evolution of the brain and the neural pathways.' (S.1.Q10) As we shall see from later communications, the neural pathways of the human brain are significant for evolution in consciousness and our perceptive faculties. Also, due to what we are now learning about neuroplasticity, it is possible to consciously, and unconsciously, engage in those practices that can rewire the neuronal pathways of the brain, thus assisting in human conscious evolution.

The Energetics of Human Evolution

The allowance of consciousness to manifest through the human being is a question of resonance and alignment. Human evolution upon this planet is also a question of correct alignment in order to move forward in balance. And this is where one of the issues facing humanity lies. As a species, we are out of balance with our environment:

> Many people are resonating below that of what the planet is resonating at and therefore out of harmony… For your own evolution it would be wise to marry the earthly energies to be in sync with that first and foremost and to connect also with the cosmic consciousness. This is your evolutionary path at present. This would then harmonise the planet and that of the cosmos too. (S.1.Q11)

First and foremost, we need to align ourselves with the earthly energies. The human species has become out of kilter with its natural vibratory environment. Humanity is in a wobble. The primary source for correcting this misalignment is humanity itself. The re-correction and realignment must come from us. It cannot be forced upon us solely from an external cause. Although the opposite is also tenable to some degree; that humanity can be compelled and nudged into greater imbalance and misalignment from external sources.

Humanity is a part of the greater cosmos, and we have the innate ability to connect – to dip in and out – of the greater field of cosmic consciousness. At the same time, since we are manifesting through a physical body, we are entitled to block this connection. It is, says Abe, just like switching the channel. And yet, just as in physical life, we cannot switch on and listen to two channels at the same time – the physical receiver can only be attuned to one channel. And this is the same with the human body. Yet the receiver can be amplified so that more of the channel broadcast can be received: 'in the future with your bodies changing to receive more and more energies then this would be possible... also, your body is limited to the energies it can receive which is a good thing. At present for to go from one state to another without progression would be detrimental.' (S.1.Q12) This is an important point as it indicates the necessity for developmental processes. Just as an electrical charge requires transformers to boost it up or lower it down, so too does the human body need 'transformer-like' processes, experiences or events that can prepare the physical body for the new energies. Otherwise, quite literally, the body could blow a fuse. The human being first needs to align with earthly energies to assist this developmental process. To put it another way, the human receptor has been covered up and we have become, to some degree, *sense blind* to our own immediate environment. As a whole, humanity is now out of synch with its natural environment, and this has resulted in a loss of functionality. Again, it could be said that we are 'in a wobble.' This loss of resonance with the home environment is causing a sickness within the human race, and this needs to be corrected immediately before greater sickness comes upon us. Abe reinforces this position: 'So, it is of utmost importance to start resonating again to your home vibration. This is done so by that inter-connect-edness, of being in nature and of bringing nature back into the system.' (S.1.Q13) For Abe to use the phrase 'utmost importance' only strengthens the necessity for this to be heeded. And what is needed is greater natural inter-connectedness. Not so much through digital communications or technologies but rather by being in contact with nature and bringing nature more into our ways of living. Modern life, Abe reminds us, has become sterile for we have moved further away from our relationship with nature and with natural forces. We have cultivated a more arti-ficial environment, and this is not conducive to our home reso-nance. There has never been a separation between humanity and its home environment; only our conditioning and social systems have taught us that this is so, and this is now causing us great dissonance.

Abe informs us that evolution is both a vibrational process as well as a material one. Life is cyclic: 'The original state is the zero-state: the zero-state is this endless becoming of form and of no form.' (S.1.Q14) This is the ongoing interweaving transition between no form and physicality. And when in physical form, our vibrations are aligned with the physical environment we are in. The correla-tion of these vibrations is what assists in the process of evolution. There is a continual shift in vibrational alignments and the recep-tivity of vibrational energies. The transference of energy needs to be as a process rather than a sudden jump. Abe explains this using the simple analogy of a home toaster:

> See a toaster - the toaster is working all well and good when the mechanism is capable of transferring the available energy to be of use to something within the environment. Higher energy for the mechanism will

blow the fuse and be of no good; too little and it will also not be in sync to do what it has to do. Do you see? (S.1.Q14)

For humanity to be in-synch with the evolutionary process it first needs to be aligned with home resonance. The next step, according to Abe, is to evolve to become more holistic. At the present time, however, the social constructs within our civilizations are making this process difficult. We are currently experiencing a struggle, and this now forms part of our process of human evolution. It is timely for humanity to reconnect with its origins/roots of wholeness. Energetic alignment is available for those who are open to it. It is not withheld. It is a question of each individual's vibratory signature that determines their state of resonance. The synching up of resonance is also a matter of being relational to it.

In light of the above, it would appear that increased urbanization is contrary to where we need to be heading. Some of this may be intentional; it is also a sign of many people having lost their resonance and 'rootedness.' Increased urbanization is also a sign of authorities wishing to administer greater control. As Abe stated: 'People and not just governments do not want to lose control never understanding that they never once had it anyway.' (S.1.Q15). The central issue here is a state of de-harmonization. And what is damaging for our external environments will only affect us in a detrimental way. If we are in a state of imbalance and de-harmonization, then whatever we do – whatever comes *from us* – will also reflect this state of disequilibrium and de-harmonization. It all comes back to us.

Our behaviour has shown that as a species we are at a young stage of evolution. In this, it is normal to be making errors and immature postures. It is this immaturity that makes us believe that we exist in separation from everything else. Because of this, there is less ongoing communication with the Continuum – we simply lack the *receptivity*. Abe confirms this: 'You are very much at a young stage in evolution compared to others, so we would say that we are not communicative with so many of your species.' (S.1.Q16) The Continuum is trying to communicate with us, whether individually or collectively, that which we already know but lays buried within. Sometimes, says Abe, we just need to wake up to ourselves.

Information such as what is being brought forth here has been put forth amongst humanity many times before, and in many ways. The time and place may be different, and this then is reflected in the manner that the information is presented or communicated; yet in essence, the core of the messages is the same. What is required for greater receptivity is a selfless openness: 'In your non-egotistical open heartedness, you can receive and that is what is happening here, a clear channel, a clear heart.' (S.1.Q17) Overall, it is a question of resonance – to be in alignment. That which is aligned comes together. Added to that is the question of time: 'What we also would like to say is that the time is right, and people are all evolving at different rates for that is the beauty of life in all its colours and diversity.' (S.1.Q17) Although there are different rates of evolution, such diversity exists within a unity – a coherence of consciousness. Abe gives the analogy of the Russian doll – the Matryoshka doll – to represent the levels of consciousness (an analogy that Abe refers to frequently): 'There are levels of consciousness; see it like this, to be that of a Russian doll – the further in you get the smaller and smaller the space. This is so with consciousness.' (S.1.Q17) Consciousness communicates through resonance; this is something that we may refer to within our common vocabulary as a form of telepathy – communication through vibrational alignment. Abe refers to this as 'the communication of the cosmos.'

The Communication of the Cosmos

Rather than anticipating, or pushing for, this type of alignment we need to open up to allow it. Here again, the concept of allowance is central: 'See, this form of communication is not something that you are making your way to but to a way in which to remember as to that in which you have always held. You have long shut out things in which are part of your being of this world.' (S.1.Q18) And why have we been blocking out these natural parts of our being? It is because we have been distracted *away from ourselves*. We have been kept outwardly occupied and stimulated by all the things which are fundamentally *not us*. And through these external distractions, humanity has been kept out of vibrational alignment: 'Vibrational alignment is and always has been an open heart, for when this is closed off, you are not able to fully communicate. You have long been lost in language. I remind you of the saying, a good old heart-to-heart. This is, it opens; this is resonance, this is truth.' (S.1.Q18) We have closed down our hearts through indulgence, or immersion, into an overly materialistic way of life. The heart vibration has been closed down as humanity became increasingly 'lost in language.' There is a reminder here of the biblical Tower of Babel story. According to Genesis, there was a united human race (generally considered to be the Babylonians) who, in their hubris, wished to create a tower to reach to the heavens. Observing this, the deity named as 'God' was concerned by these actions and decided to create multiple languages so that humans were divided into different linguistic groups and thus unable to understand and communicate with one another. And since that time, humanity has been 'lost in language.' There are many inferences to be taken from this tale, including the nature of such 'godly intervention,' yet the emphasis now should be upon wholeness and remembrance rather than speculations.

The humans upon this planet are 'but in a slumber of sorts.' This slumbering reflects our loss of alignment and correct relations: 'The way to move back into alignment is to connect with each other, with the planet, with oneself. See, it has come about that relationships are dire in all aspects of life; with your beautiful home; with yourselves.' (S.1.Q19) Many people have fallen into states of condemnation, judgement, and imbalanced relations with the world around them. And in the end, this means that we have come out of alignment with ourselves. Many true selves and emotions are not shown because of fear of what others may think and say. Many people feel pressurized into relations of competition and to show strength through power. Yet in this, we only fall into greater disharmony with ourselves. So often, we end up wasting our energies defending a false position. Each of us is now required to live our lives authentically: 'The more open your heart is the more authentic your life is, and the easy life can move through you; and in this not being continually offended by others.' (S.1.Q19)

Abe, as representing the Unified Field of the Continuum, is not separate from humanity. As such, there is a shared deep feeling for us the same as we would feel for our own families. To not have this shared feeling would be, as Abe says, like 'shutting a part out of which we are.' This cannot be so, for it would represent a splintering – and the Unified Continuum is just that: Unified. To feel, or believe, that we are communicating with something 'outside' of ourselves is only a reflection of our own splintered minds and not a reflection of the truth: 'The relationship we have is unity and for guidance from us to be able to receive comes from your own splintered mind, it is not of our separation but of yours.' (S.1.Q20) These communications are not to be regarded as guidance external to us but as from a part of our own self. We can picture it rather like the Self in conversation with the self. We may think that we are 'acting upon the world' or that 'the world is acting upon us' when the truth is that everything is interwoven in collaboration. Everything that exists is different levels of consciousness in relationality – as in the Russian doll analogy. Abe says that: 'To see the wholeness is to really be in collaboration and to be in collaboration is to be in harmony.' (S.1.Q20)

Within today's environment, saturated with impacts and influences, we tend to react (rather than responding) by closing down our hearts, and thus closing down our essential communications. By doing this we are only closing off who we really are and all that we can be. It may be said, by modern standards, that by being open-hearted and acting from our own truths that we are being selfish. Yet is this not rather living life honestly? And 'if you truly are open then you will receive much more from life.' (S.1.Q21) Through open heartedness we are receptive to these communications from further afield. Many traditions have spoken of the 'Higher Self' and yet this idea has been conceptualised as being something beyond ('higher') and away from us – as something that we need to aspire for or reach to. Yet it is not a state/place of 'highness' but rather 'an aspect of that in which you are but also an aspect to that of which we are.' (S.1.Q22) In other words: 'In communication with ABE you are indeed in communication with self.' (S.1.Q22) In our world reality there is so much division and perceptions of separation. We do this to ourselves. We divide, or allow division, to come amongst us. We also allow outside forces to create division amongst us. And in this, we lose contact with the essence of ourselves. This leads to the constant behaviour of 'othering.' There is no 'outside' or 'inside' as the cosmos is always in communication with itself – unless these communications break down, as is the case with humanity.

Relations within the greater cosmos 'is an interwoven, interconnecting vibrational web of communication.' (S.1.Q23) Through these relations, all knowledge is accessible to us. Many people in the past have been inspired by the 'music of the spheres' – the wisdom from the cosmos – and have put this out into the world in various forms: through art, philosophy, teachings, etc. It is all about the interpretation into form. And through this interpretation there can be fewer or greater filters. Abe has said: 'These greats of humanity did but one thing and they tapped into this, into us; they stopped trying and just allowed.' (S.1.Q23) Through *allowance* we can drop our filtering and facilitate the communication between Self and self. Often it is we ourselves who get in the way of this *allowance*. And that is what these communications are principally about: showing us how to get out of the way of ourselves. And in this, to find our *way back home*.

In many past instances people interpreted these communications with Self as communication with their 'God.' When knowledge, and *allowance*, is suppressed, then many things become interpreted through the limited filters of current understanding. For example, if we are wearing red-tinted glasses, then everything that we see is interpreted as with a red tint. By taking off such glasses we are dropping our own acquired filters. Our filters, such as our language, vocabulary, and concepts, more often than not get in the way of the essential truths: 'We feel that it should not be interpreted as God or Source as these words are but too much over-used and overburdened and really get in the way of that in which is truth.' (S.1.Q24) Rather than become entangled within the language and human-based concepts, Abe reminds us that what is of importance are the new 'pathways of resonance' that are being established within people. When new patterns of resonance arise, these serve to recalibrate our vibrational connections. As the saying goes: so within, so without. And this is also the case here, for internal vibrational connections will start to establish new patterns in the physical that then in turn allow the internal pathways to strengthen, and so on. Abe refers to it in this way: 'But hear this, as the pathways are built in those who are of resonance, they are making the vibrational connections; then the pathways will start to be built too in physical form and in physical form people will see and in this will allow these to be built internally.' (S.1.Q25) As each person establishes new patterns/pathways of resonance they shall be opening up their state of *allowance*. And through this state, a line of expanded communication arises between self and Self.

When asked about how to express the concept of God or Source it was revealed that the concept of unity, or unification, would be more appropriate. Specifically, the 'unification of self.' (S.1.Q26) To use terms that place this concept outside or external to us only increases the misunderstanding of separation and division which 'have caused great pain to the masses.' This 'pain' of division, Abe clarifies, relates to the 'de-harmonisation and destruction waving out as a ripple throughout all of time and space.' (S.1.Q27) The Abe material – or Continuum communications – are here to show us (or those of us who are open to consider the messages) the unity of our existence. We are being nudged to connect 'back up to that in which has been long lost.' Nothing, we are reminded, can be truly accomplished from a splintered mind.

Much has been said in the past about humanity's connection with a 'divine origin.' Over aeons of time, we have arrived at a point where many people feel more disjuncture and disassociation than ever. As Abe repeatedly says, we have become detached from ourselves – and we need to find our *way back home*. Many of our various traditions no longer correlate with their original message or purpose:

> For so much has been contaminated, like a Chinese whisper that has gone around the world far too many times and now does not correlate at all to the original words first spoken. You see, it has gotten lost in translation. (S.1.Q29)

The issue does not need to be long and drawn out or made more complicated (as is the usual tendency for humans). It is, as Abe says, more about a 'coming back.' The truth is so simple that we have overlooked it. Over time, the contaminations, or misunderstandings, accumulated so much that we were made to think the answer *had to be complex*: 'But it is not so – it is an almost unity "oh yes" and you can see and keep picking yourself up and simply bring it all back in.' (S.1.Q29)

It is time for humanity to loosen the grip upon its splintered self. Many of our traditions were useful in their time. Yet we now need to recognize that many of them have out served their usefulness. Further, that some of them are now adding to our state of splintered self and need to be let go of. The choice though can only be ours and ours alone: 'But see this, you make it as easy or hard - it is but your choice.' (S.1.Q29) There has been a plethora of information and communicated material in the past. At the core, the genuine ones all say the same thing. Now, we are being gently nudged to simplify; in other words, to downsize and declutter. Abe relates that these communications have come forth at this time 'to take it back to the bare bones.' The human species is evolving, and many people are awakening, or have already awoken, from their 'suppressed states.' Humanity has been suffering from 'an infection of mind' that is now due for healing. The communications with Continuum have come forth at this time to assist in our understanding, and to help in bringing us back to ourselves – and back to home resonance.

Each person can resist, or constrict, this alignment to home resonance; or *allow* much more through receptivity. Even the simple things are hard for us in human form, notes Abe. We tend to regard those things that come easily as of little or limited importance to us. We have become too accustomed to the struggle of life: 'You clearly need to participate in this life, but life does not have to be battled with, just met.' (S.1.Q37) The connection with Continuum does not need to be a kind of physical plugging in – to get up and 'plug in' to something. Rather, it is through *allowance of*. If we imagine that we need to somehow 'connect up' then we have 'simply lost the notion of it all together. It is but an allowance of it – to breathe, settle down, and allow.' (S.1.Q38) Each one of us is already a spiritual being; we have only forgotten our vibratory essence. It is, quite simply, a question of remembrance.

And so then, what *is* the meaning of life? The Continuum responds to us by saying: 'For the whole meaning of life is to live, and to live one must be allowing of all that you are.' (S.1.Q39) The human being is both of the physical and of the vibrational. There is no one doctrine or creed that one should live by. Yet any sense of meaning within life gets lost when looked at from a splintered mind – 'for it feels like the whole world has taken a piece of you and you are but lost within the noise outside of yourselves.' (S.1.Q39) Abe tells us that 'there would never be a dance of life if one had to do it all alone.' And so, we are urged to express ourselves in the best way possible for us. And the meaning of life is *how* we express ourselves and move through the journey of self toward Self. In the final word: 'the meaning of life - if it is to be of anything - is this EXPRESSION of but one thing... meaning of life is *you*.' (S.1.Q39)

SECTION TWO – Mind, Body & Spirit

The patterns of human understanding need to be stripped back 'to the bare bones' before we can truly be able to step forward. The human race has accumulated too much baggage; much of this in our concepts and ideas. This is also true, to a great extent, concerning our concept of the Divine: 'like we said, things need to be stripped back to the bare bones and this is so with your understanding of the divine and also of God.' (S.2.Q1) There are many people today who are not drawn to or attracted by religious terms or concepts; yet this does not negate the sense of a 'divine source' or the inner knowing of an existence greater than the individual physical human being. For many such people, a new recognition is required – a new way for them to feel connected to the grander, eternal existence. In this, Abe says: 'for the ones who are not drawn to any of these terms, and we do so feel there to be many now, we want to say that God, Divine, universe, source, are all but one thing – and you are it.' (S.2.Q1)

Everything serves a purpose at a different stage of evolution. Yet in order to move forward, older concepts and paradigms need to be constantly updated and replaced. It is somewhat similar to a baton relay race where at certain junctures the person with the baton must pass it over for the next runner to take it forward over the next stage of the course. So also, is it with concepts and paradigms of understanding; at certain junctures they need to be renewed (i.e., passed over) for the next course of the evolutionary path. If this is not done, then it comes to pass that the older concepts do not serve well the current phase. And often this realization comes too late or requires a radical turnaround to compensate for this. Older paradigms are not to be dismissed but detached from. Abe makes an analogy here between a mother and the child: 'you would not say to your mother "oh well, you gave birth to me a long time ago, you are of no use now," for we are in a large cycle in which some point you will come back to the beginning and this will be the forever becoming.' (S.2.Q2) There is some truth in most religious systems, for example, but now 'it seems that these things are driving humanity in the complete opposite direction to that of which it was intended to do so.' We need to accept this as a condition and not as a contempt for religion for these were the forms that served us for a period of our growth. As an infant grows into a child, it needs to put off the old clothes for they no longer fit the new body. Is it such a big leap to now consider/realize that the God/Source is none other than 'that in which you are'?

To put it more simply: 'You have been sleeping and it is time to wake up to that in which you are, which everything is.' (S.2.Q2) The theme of awakening has become common in modern vocabulary, especially in those circles referred to as 'New Age.' Yet the analogy is apt for we are quite literally in need of awakening from our perceptive slumber. People will always have their own beliefs and this, Abe says, is not to be dismissed. Yet what is core here is to be able to see the essential within and between all things: 'but what we want you to see, to truly see, and not just that but feel - in the core essence of your being - that even in this

world of great polarity, I see you in me and me so in that.' (S.2.Q2)
This recognition is also part of what is meant by *the way back home*.
It is about stripping everything back and returning to a 'home
vibration' and to be aligned with a home resonance. First, we
need to become in alignment with our home planet's vibration.
We have become detached and splintered from our home environment and this, principally, has caused many of our problems.
We need to unify ourselves first: 'Within a split consciousness of
"me and the world" is never going to be able to see to it that you
are a transactional vibratory essence that is not separated from
your world - more so, an expression of it.' (S.2.Q3) The human
being alters the vibration to that which it resonates with. This is
another aspect of the Abe material – that we are all transactional
beings in relation. There is no separation, and this is emphasized
more so at the energetic, or vibrational, level. Vibrational levels
are contagious; that is, they spread easily. We have a term for this
in our sciences: it is called *entrainment*. In physics it is referred to
as oscillations (i.e., vibrations) coming into "phase alignment." It
is also a term recognized in psychology that refers to "an individual's chronobiological, physical, and behavioral relationship with
their environment."[3] Knowing this, we can then understand that
when humans are in a vibrational wobble – out of balance – this
affects our physical environment through vibrational entrainment. Little wonder then that we are seeing such dissonance
and disharmony across the world today and within the planet's
natural systems. We are, quite simply, *out of synch*.

This is another reason for why the Abe/Continuum
messages have come forth at this time. Because spiritual evolution upon this planet is occurring rapidly now and this is causing
some distress with those systems that are, or cannot, be aligned

• • • • • • • • • • • • • • • • •

3   A dictionary definition

with this transformative process. There is much struggle by some elements of human society to retain the old structures, and this simply cannot be so. You cannot hold back the tide (as King Canute found out). As the planet evolves, so too does humanity pass through various degrees of spiritual development. There may have been earlier times when the human species was more spiritually aware, but now we must focus on the present times. And the central issue here is that the human species has 'been tainted by something outside of yourselves.' In other words, we have placed our authority and trust onto external agents rather than upon ourselves. Humanity has given itself away too freely. Rather than thinking we have a choice, we should trust in our own knowing. The Abe communications are about recognizing the feeling deep within us that there is truth in our own knowing, and of our relationality to Continuum: 'that you feel it deep in the core of you and resonates with you on all levels' (S.2.Q4)

This inner knowing of truth is a reflection of the consciousness that relates the human being to other expressions of consciousness, such as the planet (as well as other planets). The neural pathways within the brain are related to our vibrational resonance, and this relates us to the Earth. Abe refers often to the concept of neural pathways and how they can adapt as our vibrational signature also changes. A core understanding here is that as the Earth changes it will resonate differently, and this will trigger for itself, and also within humanity, the establishing of new vibrational patterns: 'Now hear this, as your planet evolves and morphs and changes it will resonate differently and like your internal self will also create differing pathways too.' (S.2.Q5) There have always been those people who have had the suitable neural pathways for connecting, often unconsciously, to the Unified Field of Self. In such people there has never been a loss of connection, even if they were not aware of this. Some people have naturally appeared to those around them as being 'tuned in,' as we say. Others have had this connection covered over or cloaked in some way: 'And there are others whom through evolutionary processes seem to have developed a masking of this connection and the brain develops differently.' (S.2.Q6) And yet, in all times, the connection to Continuum has always been available – and it shall always be so. Some people, it can be said, are just in deeper sleep than others.

Every person who has ever walked upon this planet has had this connection to Continuum – it can be no other way. Some people, such as those whom we have referred to as 'Teachers' or 'Masters' are those who have had a knowing, conscious contact with Continuum. This also applies to well-known teaching traditions that have expressed, in various degrees, the truths of this relation between the human being and its contact with an eternal Unity in Self. There is no need to take oneself out of life in order to maintain this contact. Of course, there may be times when too much stimulation or distraction is interfering, in which case a retreat or temporary detachment from the throngs of physical life may help. Yet, in the long term, there is no need to pull oneself out of participation with a full, physical life experience: 'The only way is to be of it and in it; there is no truth up on the hilltops but here in the midst of it all, in the polarities of existence, knowing that it is all quite ordinary but seemingly extraordinary all at the same time.' (S.2.Q8)

Life is both ordinary and extraordinary at the same time. This is part of the polarity of physical existence. Just as there is the tangible body and its intangible vibrations. The human sciences have long studied the phenomena of vibration. Perhaps in time this will come to constitute the heart of our sciences rather than the empirical drive to measure and pinpoint everything. Life will never be fully understood if it is examined through cutting it up into little pieces: 'You are human beings of your world, but it will have to always measure and dice and slice and in that will not have the full picture.' (S.2.Q9) There will need to be a merging so that the unified completeness can be seen through the physical patterns of compartmentalization. In this also, greater scientific understanding will be placed upon recognizing the vibratory nature of bodily health.

The Science of Body & Health

Vibration is at the core of everything, including how we consider human health: 'Vibration is a core essence of health care, for vibration is the language of life.' (S.2.Q10) If a person is out of vibratory alignment with their own being, then this creates dissonance within them – an out-of-synch wobble. Each manifested thing has a vibrational signature; this forms the web of communication. When we come into contact with another's vibrational signature, our own being is learning of their state – this is the same with people, food, the environment, etc. As Abe says: 'Everything has a vibrational signature, so it is true with that in which you put into your body for that is what tells the body what the outside world is like - if it is thriving or not.' (S.2.Q10) Because of this inter-relationality of vibrations it is important that we become aware of 'the vibrations of the things you put into your body' and 'that of your own vibrational signature.' This relates very well to the meaning of food and the type of food we eat. On this, Abe makes a very important point:

> You could have all the best food and eat well and exercise but if your own vibrational essence is that of lack

that you are eating this nutritious food, then you are no better off than eating all the junk in the world. For you see, there are people who are extremely fit in the world and have health problems because they are not aligned with their own vibration and that in which they are putting into their bodies. (S.2.Q10)

In regard to this, there is much healing knowledge that is simply not available to the public; or else, is being deliberately withheld from general circulation. Much of the knowledge concerning vibrational states have been retained within some authentic and/or indigenous communities yet has become largely discarded in modern cultures or put aside as being 'mystical' or 'new agey.' Modern health science has focused on the rational and logical path, and this focus has greatly supported 'health economics' yet at the detriment to overall, holistic approach to human health. Unfortunately, medication is regarded as a profitable business and there will be considerable resistance to change from within the medical industries: 'But you see, your very system has been built on such grounds now and will be difficult to re-establish without a fight of someone wanting to hold on to some sort of past.' (S.2.Q11) Such a way, however, is one-sided and this causes dissonance within the paradigm of health.

Health has always fundamentally been a personal issue, only that in recent years so many people have placed their health decisions external to them. People are losing faith and trust in making their own decisions and in following their "gut instinct." Each person instinctively knows when something is not quite right with/within them: 'You see, you know in yourselves and your bodies when something is off if you are attuned to your being, and you would know how to nurture your body back to equilibrium.' (S.2.Q12) At the same time, there is no need to be dismissive of physical life or external reasoning. It is establishing a balance between these sides, and of being observant to one's deep-seated beliefs and to be prepared to let go of ideals or ideas that are no longer sustaining or nurturing. The human body is also part of evolution, yet it does not shift to the same degree that is possible on the consciousness level. As the consciousness resonance shifts, so too must the body adapt to adjust to this. There is this correlation between body and consciousness; it is the body that houses or, rather, is a conduit for consciousness. As the vibratory rate of consciousness changes, the body vehicle will need to adapt to this. In this case, the physical body will become less dense. This inter-relation between physical density and consciousness vibration is a natural progression for they are in resonance. A certain amount of physical density is necessary to have the life expression upon the Earth. At the same time, there are periods where expansion on a conscious level becomes necessary. Humanity has entered one of those periods now: 'We want you to see that there is an expansion coming, evolutionary, that will enable your species to expand in consciousness to that in which we are. But hear this, it will always be of a density to match that of your planet.' (S.2.Q14)

Everything is in correlation and will shift to maintain the resonance. This is the way that all life evolves – person and planet. These changes occur over vast stretches of time; they are not overnight leaps. This is the way of harmonization. And yet, the shifts will not be dramatic due to the essence of planet Earth's density: 'It is always inter-relational, and you will not be of such lightness or transparency with that of your planet Earth for it is rather dense in its vibrational essence, albeit shifting.' (S.2.Q15) Humanity is not able to outgrow the planet; on the contrary, it is time to become more 'rooted' and in resonance to planet Earth: 'For the purpose of conscious evolution at this time is to put deep roots into your planet.' (S.2.Q16) If the planet is making vibrato-

30

ry shifts in which the inhabitants (i.e., humans) are not in resonance with, then life upon the planet will become increasingly
uncomfortable for its residents. Everything is inter-relational, and
this includes the planetary frequency as well as the food that is
produced and ingested. All these aspects reflect the overall health
of a person. Everything exists and participates within a 'vibrational communication system.' The intake of food also allows the
human body to know of its vibrational environment. In this way,
food, and the substances that the body absorbs from the outside,
act as vibrational information carriers. And at present, humanity
is in a vibrational imbalance:

> The current state is that it has been far way taken from
> its own harmonious balance to that of the Earth. To
> see that your Earth is suffering is to see that you your-
> selves are also suffering. You are creating a dissonance
> of vibrational communication through the toxins and
> chemicals that are being used at present and, in this,
> creating a cognitive dissonance. (S.2.Q17)

In this, we are being advised that there exist forms of vibrational
contamination. Vibrational contamination can be ingested from
external sources – from food as well as from other people. Human
societies have generally supported and praised dominant personalities. Yet such dominant people also represent dominant 'vibratory signatures' that are often out-of-synch with the required
resonance. These dominant vibratory patterns are neither good
for the planet nor for systems of inter-relating vibrations: 'but you
see, the dominant force lords it over and therefore whatever is not
allowing to meet and be of benefit to the system is not going to be
one of health or of nourishment.' (S.2.Q18)

Dominant vibratory patterns also affect the body/mind for this too is an inter-relational mechanism/apparatus for the expression of a person's 'unique vibrational essence.'

The Science of Consciousness & Mind

The human body gives a person a definitive physical shape. And yet, 'there is not a specific part of you that is in the shape of you.' Consciousness is a matter 'of connection not of form at all.' (S.2.Q20) Each person's expression of consciousness within the body-mind forms a specific 'vibratory signature' that is unique to each person. The brain acts as a filter that processes this vibratory signature. If a person's brain has been programmed with particular social conditioning, then these affectations are expressed, or given colour, through the filtering. This then results in what is termed the 'personality' or 'persona' of a given identity. The social personality is vibration given form, and people resonate with this form. The form is a 'point of attention' where the brain creates the vibrational signature we know as the mind:

> Mind is not a part of consciousness; it is a part of that which is body. It is the unseen signature, your vibrational signature, that speaks in vibrational terms and resonates. Consciousness is devoid of form - it is zero point. Mind is not consciousness but your vibrational language back to consciousness. (S.2.Q22)

And so, when the 'mind is dropped,' so to say, 'pure consciousness is allowed to flow.' Yet people have, by and large, been conditioned to identify with their personality (and ego) which then blocks or buffers against the flow of pure consciousness. But the human ego is something that we cannot detach from completely for it is part of our body-mind functioning: 'You can never but detach – it's about meeting in the middle. In the knowing of it as unification, never a one or the other.' (S.2.Q23) In this 'meeting in the middle' we can perhaps 'drop down' our human ego somewhat and consciously step back from it. It is the complete unaware attachment to ego and personality that hampers the flow of consciousness.

The flow of consciousness is central to the continuation of human evolution. By allowing the flow of consciousness we are also allowing life to move. Consciousness should not only flow but also be aligned with matter, for matter and consciousness are united – this is the 'evolutionary key.' Consciousness and matter are both forms of vibrational energy; they are aspects of the same thing – there is no separation. It is important to realize this without getting caught up in extremes; extremes of mind (meditation) and extremes of the body (materialism). The merging means to be a part of it all: 'To be feeling all this to be a part of all there is and also to be able to know the expansive truth too whilst here in physical matter – wow, what an experience. What a life. Be with it, feel it from the centre of your being, and most importantly – participate.' (S.2.Q25) Vibrations, and the vibrations of consciousness, piece existence together like a resonant web that human perception is mostly unable to grasp. It is humans themselves who, knowingly or unknowingly, close themselves off from greater vibrational communication. The more we are united with this web of vibrational communication, the more this harmonization and alignment creates expansion: 'The more available it is to you, all vibrational alignment, this web of communication will infinitely expand' (S.2.Q26)

Vibrational alignment is also related to how our individual brains are wired. And people's brains develop differently in main part to their exposure to different forms of social conditioning. Certain social conditioning of the brain blocks out natural connectivity; and some of this blockage has been deliberate. Why, we may wonder: 'how would they be able to sell your parts back to you if they do not firstly recondition and break it apart in the first place?' (S.2.Q27) Humanity has been 'coaxed' into playing a game it is largely unaware of; and we have thought 'that it is indeed what life is all about.' But this is not the truth, for there is so much more to life. However, for many people, the 'wiring is all wrong.' And through this social wiring – life's programming – so many people have been hypnotized: 'for you have been hypnotized by the highs of modern-day society and when coming back to this it all seems rather dull, rather un-special. But you will see that the one who is awake will indeed see the extraordinary within the ordinary.' (S.2.Q27) Part of the 'wiring is all wrong' syndrome contributes also to the 'depression epidemic' that symbolizes the dissonance. This is because 'people feel torn between vibrational alignment and the rewiring of the vibrational alignments of the brain. In this you see that now too depression can be a false premise to keep you in this game also...' (S.2.Q27)

It must be recognized that there are some people, or power groups, that utilize these processes to manipulate people and to keep them in perceptual slumber. At the same time, there are many people who show no interest in awakening from their slumber: 'and it is also so that people are set - they are not at all interested in getting out of their seats for they have all that they need right here, do they not? Why question it?' (S.2.Q28) There are those who are happy and content to have the food on their table and do not wish to rock the system beyond this. Of such people, Abe says: 'For some will go an entire lifetime and have never lived a single true moment in their entire life. What a shame. What a waste.' (S.2.Q28)

Another side of human conditioning is the conditioning of our emotions. All vibrations are *felt*; they are then filtered through our mind and transformed into 'a thing.' We make separate 'things' from our emotions; we give them conditions, rules, and categories. These 'things' can then be exploited and manipulated by outside events (media) or other persons. We should be more aware of attaching these *felt vibrations* onto external objects and things; for it is then these external objects which can reverse engineer our own feelings. The bottom line is this: we should embrace being human – it is important that *we are humans*. After all, this is the whole point of having this life experience: 'Humans have flaws and accepting them is a way to resonate higher.' (S.2.Q32) People often cause their own discomfort by struggling to be 'somewhere higher' when in fact 'it is all here and only the splintered mind cannot see.' We are currently human; and at the same time, we 'are a long track of vibrations and matter and endless cycles of life and form.' (S.2.Q32) Knowing this, how can anyone truly be splintered? Life and consciousness are aspects of an undivided beauty. Everything already *is*.

In the physical existence, however, all vibration 'is distorted in some way or another.' It is our inner purpose, if one can call it that, to shift into a unity resonance. Each individual 'vibrational signature' is made up of many differing vibrations and yet, as Abe says – 'make one like water that passes through a sieve - whole, separated and whole again.' (S.2.Q33) Our band of vibrations (our 'signature') may have differing vibratory aspects, and yet we can bring them into wholeness. The pure stream of consciousness flows through the human body and is filtered and interpreted by the human brain. This consciousness flow is 'transformed' according to the conditioned programming of the brain (our 'filters'). The result is a person's unique vibrational signature. Yet what we express in our lives is a coloured or 'transformed' aspect of the pure consciousness: 'What we are really trying to say is yes, the vibration is always changed by your own vibrational signature.' (S.2.Q33) The aim then, if there is one, is to allow this stream of source consciousness to flow more directly through us and into life – this represents the 'universal flow.' Using again the analogy of water, a water filter (the person) may have contaminants that affect the purity of the water; and this is a hindrance. So, says Abe: 'why not drop the filter, allow pure consciousness to flow by cutting out the unnecessary middleman. This does not mean to be pushed around and passive, but to have direct experience with life.' (S.2.Q33) There will always be, and always have been, people who try to manipulate this energy flow for their own ends and means. Yet this cannot be done if people do not submit to these manipulations – everything is part of the whole. The wholeness is the end and beginning of all things – the *alpha* and the *omega*.

In the Continuum there is nothing 'beyond' for it is that which holds ALL: 'we are where all form is and where all form is born from and will eventually fall back too.' (S.2.Q34) All existence, all forms of life, are within this wholeness – the Unity. We all share from the same consciousness. We are the Continuum, and the Continuum is us. When within the dense physical life expression, we restrict this flow by being too engrossed in our own vibration. As in the analogy of the Russian dolls, humanity confines itself into the smallest of the dolls and we hypnotize ourselves into this bubble of limited vibration. Yet as everything is essentially an aspect of Continuum, then it is almost as if everything in existence is having a conversation with itself: 'Like the whole universe is mad, talking to oneself.' (S.2.Q36) And at the same time, 'there can be a myriad of expressions of just one thing. How wonderful that is to see.' We are urged to allow more of this; to allow 'more in' by 'letting up.' In other words, by letting up our ego-identity restraints. Life is not terrifying, we are told. On the contrary, it is 'but a great expression of one thing and you can go ahead and just live, just participate.' (S.2.Q36) We often restrict ourselves through fear – fear of the loss of self. How irrational and contradictory this now seems: we fear a loss of self by allowing Self to flow. Throughout our human history we have wanted to prove that 'I am me' and 'I exist' when we were in fact only strengthening our false, or lesser, identities. If only people could 'just let this go a little they will see that there is so much more to be open to, so much more to be receiving.' (S.2.Q37)

It can be said that artists, such as writers and inventors, are people in whom there is a greater flow of this pure consciousness. The 'muse,' as it has been called, is this inspiration gained from allowing the Continuum to flow through one's vibratory signature. Great ideas have been seeded into human civilization through the creations of artistic people. There has always been such 'open' people who have served as conduits for this consciousness flow to merge into material expression. Once this was referred to as the 'gift of the gods.' In this, 'the whole universe talking to itself to be able to know itself. These things set in motion as little pointers to wake you up like alarm clocks dotted all about the universe.' (S.2.Q39) And it is important that we realize 'of how great and wonderful it really is to be in form.' We are being urged now to become grounded – within ourselves and with our environment. Before we should go any 'higher' we first need to come back to ourselves. For example, so many people speak of a 'higher consciousness' and this inevitably makes us think of going out of ourselves towards another state. Yet, as Abe explains: 'Higher consciousness is indeed that way, not a higher place to get to but a resonance in which you are more accustomed to be - more open to receive.' (S.2.Q43) Perhaps we should replace the term 'higher consciousness' with 'receptive resonance.' Again, this does not mean we need to seek out for a particular resonance, as if going on a search party. First and foremost, it is 'of the notion of coming to grips with that in which you are. There is never anywhere to get to, just a knowing of that this is how it is.' (S.2.Q43)

There is the risk that in going too far away from ourselves we may in fact be causing greater dissonance. It is a human trait that we feel compelled to seek solutions and answers outside of ourselves; and in doing this, we trigger greater imbalance and dis-ease within ourselves.

Human Health, Disease & Dissonance

The human body has been experiencing increased dissonance in recent years. Some of this has come from our diets, the types of food we eat, as well as the chemicals used in modern food production. And yet everything we do is a reflection of our own states; and this includes how we produce and consume food. The origin of our errors is our own lack of self-understanding: 'if you really could understand yourselves then you would indeed not want to put the things you do so into your bodies.' (S.2.Q45) The food we intake mixes with our vibrational alignment. And with the rise of genetically modified food use there is the increase in vibrational modification. All these vibrations ripple out and also affect the planet as it is always inter-relational: 'It needs to be more open and understanding of these vibrational essences of life and the inter-relational connection of everything.' (S.2.Q46) We will never get a true grasp on the meaning of health until we first come to realize and acknowledge that we are vibrational beings. We can take care of the 'mechanics' but we also need to take care of our vibrational signature: 'This meaning, you also take on the vibrational signature of that in which you eat.' (S.2.Q47) As the maxim goes: Garbage In; Garbage Out. If the food we put into us is of low quality – i.e., low vibration – then this will affect the vibratory state of the body. It is important then that we become aware that as humans we are vibrational as well as physical.

Disease also comes by way of addiction, which is a reflection of seeing the world as disconnected. There are many false ideas and ideals in the world that create dissonance. People often feel stressed and pressured to live up to one belief, ideal, concept, or another. And for some people, they wish to escape from this energy of dissonance and disconnect. And there are many forms that this escapism can take. Some people 'are maybe obsessed with changing lovers or addicted to food or sex or working. See, anything can be an addiction in a sense, to escape this life. I suppose it is just what people are going to choose as their vice.' (S.2.Q48) The bottom line is that vibrational dissonance causes disease; and this is as true whether for addiction or for cancer. As Abe says concerning disease: 'It always starts off as dissonance, always.' (S.2.Q49) Disease, of course, can lead to death; and death is one of the most misunderstood concepts within humanity. It is also a subject that creates great fear within many people. There is nothing wrong in mourning for a departed friend or loved one. This is also part of being human. We need to allow this grief to come up and to be expressed, if this is what is necessary. As Abe reminds us in such times: 'You do not need to become unattached to life. You see, in the beauty of that heartfelt release of another, you feel alive. That is beauty, that is part of being human.' (S.2.Q50)

Death is not the end. The body is left behind, yet the vibrational signature that is 'you' continues on. And without the physical body, there is no further splintering: 'When you have no body you are no longer splintered - you are back to wholeness, that is it.' (S.2.Q50) The knowing that physical death is a transition stage rather than an end can profoundly alter how people live and view their lives. The understanding of the transition through death is critical. It is a change in form; and the human form is part of a cycle that comes from wholeness and returns to wholeness. As Abe says: 'There is deep beauty in this process. There has been much fear around death, and it is understandable in a way as your mind works in the polarities of life.' (S.2.Q51) The human vibrational essence is a part of this wholeness and not apart from it. Life is a process and throughout this process there are different stages, and these stages will also take differing forms. The vibrational essence that is the 'You' will no longer be sustained within a physical body after the death process. Nothing is lost; everything is retained: 'a wholeness in life or consciousness constantly expressing itself, constantly talking to itself.' (S.2.Q51)

In one sense, the wholeness that we are a part of has lived, and will live, all lives. Existence can be said to be cyclic in that there is this continuation of form and no-form; but this is a different concept than reincarnation. The concept of reincarnation has been tainted by religious connotations, especially the idea that a person's 'soul' must keep returning in order to learn lessons to 'get it right:' 'religion imposed the idea of a cycle coming back and back until you finally get it right. There is some truth in a sense that life is cyclic, but no truth in that it is to get this life right.' (S.2.Q52) The moral implications were imposed by human minds. In essence, there is the continuation of existence through countless expressions of form and no-form: 'Life moves, life cycles, life is change and life is consciousness.' (S.2.Q53) Although in human physical form we have to come to new understandings, in essence we already are what we are: the human self 'does not have to reach a higher state for it to be accepted with open arms and to say "good job."' (S.2.Q53) The point of being here now is to awaken to that which we already are. What this means is that we are not here in a human life expression to learn how to become 'better in essence' or to become something 'other' than what we already are – we are here to be an aware expression of that which we already are. Abe gave a simple yet elegant story to express this, which is worth citing in full. Here it is:

> a baby kangaroo abandoned by his mother was taken in by a pack of hyenas. Now all was good and well until one day the grown kangaroo bumped into another kangaroo. The other kangaroo hopped off and the kangaroo was in awe of this creature. He went about trying to be like the kangaroo but could not be, until one day the hyenas came clean and he was told that he too was a kangaroo like the one he had seen and in that moment of knowing he was able to hop and jump just like the others. (S.2.Q53)

It is not about learning lessons but more about remembrance – about *knowing*. It is 'like connecting back up the phone line that you had left off the hook.' It is poignant that the Continuum, through Abe, tells us that we always have everything we need – and therefore all we really need is to see this. In the zero state, everything is wholeness. Imagine this wholeness as a single flower. In form, each life expression is as a petal; and each petal has its own unique, distinct scent even though it comes from the same unified flower.

It is within the splintering that dissonance arises; and from dissonance comes disease. Vibrational dissonance can occur when different vibrations are rejecting or repelling one another. In this instance, there is no harmonization or attraction. Similarly, there can be a vibrational contamination from a dominant or heavy vibration: 'See this, when you walk into a room and there has been an argument you feel the density in that room. You feel as though your whole being is weighted upon - this is the true meaning of dark energy.' (S.2.Q55) Dissonance is caused when two different vibrations are trying to be held at the same time – there is a mismatch. Abe gave a simple explanation:

> Take it like this, you hate broccoli. You had a bad experience and was extremely sick when you were a child eating some. Now the doctor comes along and says that broccoli is the only thing that will make you better today. You have complete vibrational dissonance. See, life as you experience it and in this your own vibrational signature is being wound together. (S.2.Q55)

The human body speaks to itself vibrationally, and in this communication there needs to be harmony. The bodily vibration needs to be in resonance to 'that of which you are' – i.e., your vibrational signature – as well as with the environment. This is important when we connect it to our diets. As mentioned previously, when the body ingests something from the outside (such as food) this informs the body of the external vibrational state. If a person ingests some factory-processed food, which is vibrationally dead, then this communicates to the body's cells that the external environment is like this – vibrationally dead. And in this case: 'the vibrational signature will be lowered because it tells the cells to act in a certain way.' (S.2.Q55) Thus, by having a bad diet, such as based on factory-processed food, a person is lowering their immune system and their vibrational state. And this also works the other way around too. If a person eats only organic food and yet their internal vibration is not a match for this, then this too creates dissonance. All in all, there needs to be a vibrational match – a resonance. Abe gave a telling example here:

There was a lady whom only ate fresh organic fruits and vegetables, never smoked or drank, exercised regularly, and still died at the age of 35 from a heart attack. This was because her vibrational dissonance was caused by the vibrational signature she had due to her heartache. She was so focused on her health and wellbeing she forgotten about her relationships, and in this she felt that dissonance in her heart. Life is always about balance - always. (S.2.Q55)

Dissonance can also occur when we block ourselves from the flow of life. The more open that people are to this flow of life (pure consciousness), or Continuum, then the more they let go of their constricting minds. For when there is more space, so to say, then things are allowed to move. It is our constricting minds which are often blocking us from seeing greater truths – such as in the case of human DNA.

At one point, the sciences referred to a great portion of the human DNA as 'junk.' This was a quite ridiculous concept, and it showed that human scientists had not yet understood how to 'decode that at which they are not open to.' In fact, human DNA is very much the vibrational code of life - it is vibrational memory: 'For in this vibrational code you have all the knowledge of who you are.' (S.2.Q56) DNA is also a receiver of vibrational code, like a body-antenna. In this, each person carries the vibrational code from where we have come from, via our parents; yet we can also 'receive new DNA structure by opening up to this one consciousness.' This is, after all, how evolution functions. Humanity can allow itself to evolve forward through receiving new vibrational codes into its DNA. In other words, a 'memory bank' of evolution is programmed into human DNA, similar to how a computer would receive a new software update. This update would come in the form of a different resonance that would then bind, or merge, with the existing one to form a new DNA resonance: 'For when new DNA is then created it is binding together what is two resonances and creating but one new; and one could say and hopefully would be improved, evolved.' (S.2.Q57) There are some people who continue to place power outside of themselves and engage in 'new agey' practices for such things as 'DNA activation' when there 'really is no need for this.' As Abe says, such practices 'do awaken people to be more open, but many get so caught up in it.' (S.2.Q59) DNA is not only Earthbound or unique to this planet – it is a cosmic code: 'It is the code of life on all planets and works exactly the same for all species all over the cosmos.' (S.2.Q60) Even some scientists have supported this idea through the concept of panspermia. This hypothesis proposes that cosmic bodies such as comets can transport DNA through space and between planets within certain life forms, such as bacteria. The Nobel-prize scientist, and co-discoverer of DNA, Francis Crick went one step further and supported the hypothesis of *directed panspermia*. This suggests that microorganisms, as cosmic carriers of DNA, are deliberately sent (or transported) through space – such as by an advanced extra-terrestrial civilization – to seed new planetary systems, or to seed lifeless planets.

At this current stage, humanity is in the process of shifting away from a physical evolution and more into a conscious evolution. In this, DNA will act as a receiver of vibration (vibrational codes) enabling this process and to 'bring together' the necessary resonance. All this is part of the expression – the dance – of life. Further, these new vibrational resonances will create new neural pathways and thus new connections. This will affect the structure of the human physical body: 'Your bodies will not be so dense as the vibrational essence rises on your planet, and in this will allow the system to thrive for longer.' (S.2.Q62) As part of this 'vibrational evolution' – an evolution in consciousness – the human body will live longer for 'the body will not be so pressured.' The human body then is set to thrive or gain a life extension. This will concern also how our societies and cultures will relate and respond to the human body living for longer.

SECTION THREE – Human Society & Culture

I t is a standardized human trait that we seek verification from outside sources. Even when we leave school a part of us remains as a schoolchild. We accept facts and information from external sources without questioning. We accept what we have been told about our histories, our culture, other cultures. We have come to regard everything that is 'not us' to have to be outside of us. In other words, there is *us* and then there is *everything else.* If something is not physical or tangible for us, then we tend to dismiss its existence or relevancy. These are the limitations that we impose upon ourselves: 'You only limit yourselves by shutting out that in which you are.' (S.3.Q1) Everything is in flux, in constant motion. This includes the cycles of civilization as well as natural phenomena across the planet. By limiting ourselves to physical materialism and patterns of stability, we lose access to the vibrations and frequency that accompany these periods of change. And we are engaged in one of those periods right now:

> Your planet and the cosmos are in constant flux, and
> the ones who resist and hold so tightly to what they
> believe, and cannot move forward with this, will surely

not be able to keep their own heads above water due
to the new vibrations, due to this new energy. (S.3.Q1)

Vibrations are 'new' to us in a physical sense – in how and when
we experience them through our physical bodies. We have
entered a planetary moment where such 'new vibrations' and
energies are manifesting more intensely. As is always the case,
there are those who choose to resist such 'moments' and struggle
to retain the old patterns. This is usually those people who have
vested interests in the older ways, or those who are not amena-
ble to (or have been conditioned against) change. Destructive
openings also bring opportunities for growth: 'when the seed is
cracked open it could be seen as completely destructive, when
in essence it is bringing new life.' (S.3.Q2) New life will need to
crack open the old shell in order to come forth. Only when we
view these things in separation, in isolation, do they seem dark or
negative. These are the times now for grounding this new energy
– for *allowing* it to merge into this reality. As more of this energy
flows into this reality, the more shall it sweep away the vestiges of
the old. By holding onto the outgoing energy, we attach ourselves
and become entangled in old patterns that no longer serve us.

The more we ground this new energy, the more disturbance that will initially be felt: 'To answer if there is increased
disruption, we would say yes; as there are many that are grounding this vibration.' (S.3.Q2) And yet the disruptions will be felt
more in those systems that can no longer hold the new energies.
For those people, groups, and systems moving into the new
energy, the disturbance is not for them or part of their space.
By seeing more disruption, we are also recognizing that 'more
people are enabling unification.' There is no special science here,
no specific roadmap or blueprint. It is first in the *allowance* of being
who you are by living without all the accumulated baggage. We

are not stagnant beings but awareness in a flow with itself. Life is a 'united field of existence.' We must step away from our robot selves programmed by endless social conditioning and feel into our own truths. If people can do this, then 'change will manifest in even the darkest of corners and it will light up all that is still hiding in the shadows.' (S.3.Q3)

Often, we need to loosen our grip on things – not just physical things but also those things that our minds become attached to. Also, our language: 'your mind gets lost in the language - in the naming and pinpointing of particular things.' (S.3.Q4) Like a narrow pinpoint of limited sight, we become lost in our own myopic short-sightedness. It is as if looking at the pebbles but not seeing the road. There can be a greater connection in expansion – in opening up to the flow. All our language and beliefs are based on human structures, even when they are religious-orientated ones. Each civilization had its own structures; every civilization understood the passing of time differently and had their own notions for explaining cycles. Life is cyclic, yet we can easily get caught up in one specific interpretation over another. In this, as Abe says: 'you are forever becoming but never getting to see things.' (S.3.Q6) As humans we tend to pinpoint one thing whilst neglecting others. It all depends on where our focus is at the time. In this, we are stopping and starting, or starting over, instead of interacting with the change and 'morphing.'

Planetary Evolution

Evolution is change. Evolution is always vibratory. Vibrations interact within other vibrations – fields within fields (again referring to the Russian doll analogy). Evolution across the spheres is tightly inter-woven: 'For you to have your own planetary evolution, it has a knock-on effect to other places in the cosmos.' (S.3.Q7) This is, according to Abe, part of 'the pattern of the forever becoming.' And as everything is inter-woven, then so too is humanity intertwined with the state, and fate, of the planet. Many people are concerned with the state of the planet, and yet they only consider the implications from a physical perspective. The physical side of things, we can say, is of the lesser path: 'yes, you can interfere, but not so much in a way of physical action. It needs to be of this conscious, this vibratory action.' (S.3.Q8) The realm of affect, rather, is from vibratory action. There will be those who would dismiss this understanding as they are invested in making physical action and gaining self-satisfaction from their outward actions. There is a time for both – for action and no action – yet these need to be considered and not just taken as matter of fact.

As evolution is vibratory it would make sense that greater participation can occur through a conscious awareness of these processes: what has generally been referred to as *conscious evolution*. To be conscious is to facilitate this merging, or the allowance, with unified field consciousness: 'It is an allowing of pure consciousness to be present in this time-space reality.' (S.3.Q9) Only the physical body can be tangibly present in this 'time-space reality.' And so, the pure consciousness would merge with the individual's vibratory signature. These differing vibrations would come together and manifest through the body: a merging of matter and spirit. If, or when, we are not conscious then our vibratory signature is running the show through the unconscious. It is fair to say that for the majority of people, the vibratory flows are operating without their knowing: 'you can be unaware and lost in the unconscious, never knowing that there is so much more to your being.' (S.3.Q9) By allowing the greater field of consciousness to flow through us into this time-space reality we are in fact supporting the evolutionary process upon the planet. And yet, ironically, people are resisting evolution: 'You need to stop resisting evolution.' (S.3.Q10) When a person is in allowance, they instinctively know what the right way to be is. As things stand, most of humanity are distorting this flow. The analogy that Abe makes is that of 'light hitting any physical thing, it will bounce off in all directions.' (S.3.Q11)

Everything is inter-related within the Continuum, for everything *is* Continuum. As such, physical-material manifestations have related influences upon one another, most of which are beyond human perception and comprehension. When there is energetic dissonance upon this planet, such as through atomic/nuclear explosions, then these energetically ripple out through the Continuum. In this respect, 'what you do is only but done upon you.' (S.3.Q12) The energy of the Unified Field – the energy available throughout the cosmos – can be tapped into anywhere. Some sites were specifically constructed across the planet (especially in ancient history) to enable this connection to, and utilization of, Source-Continuum energy. Some of these sites are known to us as their remnants still exist. Many other sites remain unknown for either they have left no physical traces or because they were not manifested physically. Certain places became as 'portals' because the intention to connect was built into them: 'only because they built up the intention to connect in a certain spot did it become a portal or a place to connect.' (S.3Q14) In the Continuum, each place is a part of the unified energy field and therefore is 'connected.' It is not possible for contact with the Continuum to exist 'here' but not 'there.' There is no outside or inside as boundaries and separations are those things physically created as external aspects of the Continuum – or rather, as aspects of the simulation within the Continuum. Connection is built-up through intention. If there is a concentration of intention, such as in a place of worship or a sacred site, then the energy of contact can be sensed more readily: 'It can be felt because of the people and the resonance of connection, not because of the place.' (S.3.Q15) That is, intention establishes a greater 'resonance of connection.' For this reason, specific places are created to gather this intentionality and to foster it.

Across the planet there are also many specific pathways – often also pilgrim routes – that connect physical sites and locations. These can be likened to planetary neural connections that have a vibrational resonance, as if creating a vibrational membrane upon the planet. Topics such as these, and many more, are so difficult to discuss openly in most cultures – especially in modern 'developed' societies. Why is this? Why are people censoring themselves? Much of this comes from the heavy social conditioning that is placed upon people as they grow up within their cultures. Realities are programmed into us along with their narratives. Many subjects are 'taboo' for us because, as Abe says, 'you do not understand yourselves.' If humans knew themselves better, then such subjects would not be beyond our normal ken of discussion and recognition. Yet it is we who place these topics outside of ourselves. Again, the sense of division is what comes from us. People create their own 'taboo zones' and places of fear where they do not wish to go. These are false, artificial boundaries for they have been constructed from human imaginings: 'For humans think that they have to impose their way only because they are not consciously aware.' (S.3.Q17) Why would we assume that other, more evolved, species in the cosmos would think the same way as us. If they have evolved further, then it is because they are aligned with the unified field and understand the nature of life within the Continuum. If humanity wishes to continue further along its evolvement in a balanced way, then we too need to open up further to these resonant energies and the larger fields of consciousness. Life, we are informed, is 'one of cyclic motion.'

Our Social & Cultural Systems

Human nature has aligned itself with a pattern of consumption that is ingrained in our social systems. The issue that troubles us today is that these patterns of consumption have been monopolized by certain groups that operate through greed. In this there also needs to be a shift towards a rebalancing. Consumption is related to resources, and this is a relationship that needs to function through correct alignment and harmony; otherwise, energies unravel and create dissonance. The planet Earth is good at bringing imbalances back into alignment – although, this is less pleasant for those of us living upon her surface. What is required here, as in all things, is awareness: 'Really, all you need to be is aware - the planet knows its own balance like you do with your own body, if you are aware.' (S.3.Q18) Yet humans tend to view resources through the lens of monetization. This is a lower form of resource understanding and, naturally, only allows for growth to a certain stage and not beyond. Humanity has reached the threshold of these lower limits. The rebalance will come when people awaken to this situation: 'But you see, it does balance itself back out when people awaken and connect.' (S.3.Q18) Natural balance within humanity is in relation to awareness. It is all connected to how aware and perceptive we are, and our openness to the flow of pure consciousness, or Source connection.

A key relation in the physical world is between people and resources. At the current time, a major issue is that of population trends. There has been a progressing trend of people moving into cities and the expansion of urban areas. Across the world there is the expansion of metropolises into megalopolises that house many millions of people. This urban movement has been promoted, and encouraged, by the major global governing bodies. In fact, it is part of their publicly stated objective. The central issue, however, is not numbers or social management but balance: 'We always come back to it, but balance is key, and people to resources is of essence.' (S.3.Q19) Whether it is overcrowding people together or manufacturing foods that do not nourish, it is all related to imbalance. Everything has 'become quick and more' and this creates dissonance and disharmony. There are governing agencies across the planet that are attempting to put new systems into place to deal with rising population. These agendas are now being heavily contested for they appear to be representations of nefarious forces. And these forces are not showing compatibility, or resonance, with the new energies that need to come in for human evolvement: 'this new energy that is upon your civilization has to resonate to that of the system. If not, you will not be able to go forward in this physical existence.' (S.3.Q19) This is an important point here. If the human systems that are being put into place in our societies do not resonate to the new incoming energy, then humanity upon this planet 'will not be able to go forward in this physical existence.' The need for resonance is paramount.

Another important point here is that political systems across our various societies are largely corrupt. People have been losing faith and trust in the political establishment for some time now. The political systems are also a part of the necessary transformation; a point that Abe agrees with. Furthermore, Abe reminds us that as people awaken to this corruption and programming, they will push back:

As more and more people awaken, they will see that indeed things are not in balance, are off. Like you have been so conditioned in a way. As more and more people come back round, in a sense they will see. But see this, people will be outraged and disappointed and angry like they have been betrayed and hypnotized and befooled, and you will see all this mayhem and pushing back. You know, we like to say that you can never fight the old by fighting it. (S.3.Q20)

As always, we are told that it is important not to play into the same game – not to step onto the same playing field. The point here is not to 'fight the old' by using the same energy but rather to step into a new energy. When we fight against the old, we are only keeping it there, upholding it by recognizing it. We need to take away our recognition – to withdraw our energy from it. The present corrupt and imbalanced systems would prefer that we react to them. By enticing us to react, resist, and argue, they are keeping our focus on them, which then continues to feed them and validate their existence. As Abe says: 'We really want you to claim all yourselves back before you can take a step forwards - to action this is our purpose and it is also yours.' (S.3.Q20)

It now seems that many social and cultural systems are in for an overhaul. The question is whether they will go through a transformation into systems that are balanced and in resonance with humanity's evolvement; or whether they will move into increased corruption and dissonance. Another of these major systems is the economic one, and the global financial system. The transformation from physical currencies into digital ones is already underway. As ever, there will be those few who will try to manipulate this change to benefit them over others: 'There will be people who claim more and channel it in a way so that it benefits a few manipulating and directing this system.' (S.3.Q21) Yet Abe also informs us that 'as more people get wise to this, the more they can claim it back.' And this is the point: people need to claim back their sovereignty, their rights. It is by coming together that people can collectively harness their innate power: 'many coming together is a lot more powerful than the one holding the bunch of notes alone. They will not have power or place to manipulate if people unite.' (S.3.Q21) And this is precisely why the few continue to 'keep things splintered.' They aim to disconnect people from one another. Yet when united we are an incredible force.

Money is a form of energetic exchange. As an energy of exchange, it functions better when it is being circulated rather than accumulated. Our sense of the energy and utility of money also needs to be re-conditioned, so we view it as a source and energy of vitalization and possibility, and not as a means of greed and control. The fallacy of money has been placed upon us, and from this we need to break free. Many people are already waking up to the dissonant and unethical nature of our national and global systems. Yet there are more still who remain asleep within the 'trap of consumerism and political disconnection, thinking that always they have to pick a side when there is no side to pick and all is worn out.' (S.3.Q23) The reason for these communications, for the Abe messages, is to assist many people in gaining awareness of this situation sooner that we might have: 'For if left too late, everything else will have been completely exhausted.' (S.3.Q23) It is when a person is not awake that they seek control. A person of genuine awareness will have no need for the energy of domination. For this reason, it can be said that many social systems are being pushed into a controlling agenda. Yet, for every act of suppression there is a counter-energy: 'this pressing something down, it will at some point have no other choice but to bounce back.' (S.3.Q24) This is the tug-of-war situation between these energetically opposed energies.

As forms of propaganda and social conditioning continue, and even increase, so also will there be a rising wave of awareness about human sovereignty and individual power. This is the 'pushing and pulling' that we are to expect in these times. We cannot expect life to be 'euphoric.' As Abe reminds us: 'If there is a heaven then it is here with you now, and the same with hell.' (S.3.Q25) Everything is here with us now. And if we believe in a heaven and a hell, then that is also here with us, so to speak. What this means is that we have to deal with all these issues and unpleasantness here during our physical life experience – not to put it off into some imagined future. We need to see all that 'in which you truly are.' Too much of the time we are being tossed to and fro by cultural slogans that say we are one thing or tell us to do another thing. Abe likens this to us being sold our own fragments: 'Society does indeed dumb you down and cut you into so many pieces for if it didn't so, then how would they be able to sell you your fragments back?' (S.3.Q25) The human transformation, including our social and cultural systems, will only come about from having a realization of the situation we are in. And this includes a realization and perception of ourselves. For indeed: 'if you do not break such a constricted pattern of being, then how will you ever see any change?' (S.3.Q26) If we continue to act and behave from the same patterns, then how can we expect to break this continual chain? This is how the status que maintains itself, from perpetuating the same patterns that keep it in place.

Change may be uncomfortable at first. This is the energy felt when old patterns are broken in order to be replaced by the new. There are always those people who prefer to deny these changes, and there is great shame in this:

it is much easier to sit back down and numb-out again because people are so afraid to feel, to love, and to live. What a shame! If only they knew that – wow – this is what I can do. I feel hurt but in this I am alive, I am here, I am participating. Such beauty in this realization. (S.3.Q27)

There is much to be said about this form of participation in life – participation in the changes. Society is in need for its inhabitants to connect and unite. This is what the social body is for: it is a body that needs for its limbs to work together, harmoniously, and in unity. This is the true use of our global technologies of communication – to unite us. Or rather, to show us externally, physically, how we are to be connected so that we exist in this way without dependencies on such technologies: 'for people who are able to adapt to this new energy or allowance there will not be such a need for these physical technologies.' (S.3.Q28) Abe informs us that this state is still some time away, yet we should understand that the human being is a vibrational part of this communication flow: 'the heart is the connector vibrationally and the head is the receiver - just like a phone line. If these are both open to receive then it will be that way.' (S.3.Q28)

The energy of unity amongst us is powerful; so powerful that it could successfully energize a harmonious planetary civilization. And yet, we are moving towards global governance (a global government?) through an energy of dissonance, fragmentation, and control – and this is the danger. In the ideal state, humans would not need a structure of government lording it over them: 'then we would hope that there would be no need to be governments but just humans.' (S.3.Q29) One of the first steps, as has already been mentioned, is that people need to break free from their layers of social conditioning. Human society is based upon social conditioning, and this will not allow us to evolve in the direction we need to take. Abe is quite clear on this: 'Your human society is but built upon social conditioning. It really does take you further down the rabbit hole. Its outdated structure is just that – outdated. It does not and will not resonate with the new wave, the new vibration. (S.3.Q30) Again, the dissonance comes from when we hold onto outdated structures – we need to let go. Yet there are those few who take the contrary position and seek to maintain, and even advance, these older structures in their path of control. Change, however, *is* coming. People are feeling, are sensing, the 'winds of change.' Only that, for now, so many are not sure what this 'change' is or how it will come about. This is why the Abe communications have manifested at this time:

> This is where we would like to come in and lend a helping hand or more, so both in physical form, this connection – these words – will resonate with many, for we wanted to get it down to the bare bones again, no nonsense. The way to de-condition is by needs of allowing this flow of energy. Allowing the heart to open and allowing the mind to be free. (S.3.Q30)

This is where the work lies, for many minds – and many hearts – have become closed down. We are in need of opening up to ourselves; and opening up to Source connection. This is how life in the Continuum should be.

Within our limited perspectives we are still clinging to outdated identities; to closed groupings and affiliations which perpetuates a politics of separation. Part of this is fear – a fear of loss: 'people live a lot in fear – in fear that people will take what they have, their status, their belongings, their identity. When they feel threatened in this way they fight back and want to claim what is rightfully theirs.' (S.3.Q31) This state of insecurity is propagated and upheld by our media, news, and political systems for it sustains nationalism, needful belonging, and identity rivalries.

These identity separations serve as limiting vibrational patterns that keep people closed down and not receptive to the flows of expansive consciousness. Also, these patterns and energies of separation keep people dependent upon their social and cultural systems and less self-sufficient. We see this reflected in our living habits. Many choices are made for modern comforts and conveniences. People like to be within cities, near to entertainment or restaurants – to have their needs nearby. And although there are many connections available in such environments, there is still a noticeable lack of community. Connections are transient, superficial, or based on transaction rather than on tangible bonds and friendship. This is going to become more noticeable as shortages or restrictions begin to arise. It is important then that we cultivate contact with the natural spaces around us as we nurture the spaces within us.

Sustainable lifestyles and living patterns may not be for the majority, yet they bring great benefit: 'we would like to see it more community focused for it not only gives connection to your world but to each other - working together, cultivating together, sharing the food.' (S.3.Q33) Many people are already strangers to their neighbours, and this does not support the energies of connectivity and community. It is likely that more alternative-style communities will arise as current living patterns deteriorate in sustenance. This may then develop into 'a gathering of communities working together.' Such communities are likely to be more attractive once there is a shift away from, or a breakdown in, our present global currencies:

> 'You will see this far more so when your currency that you have now is no longer of use. You see, people think that in this sense of doing this you will be taking a step backwards. But it is not so. There will be deeper

connection in this to your world, to each other, and also
to that of your instinctual human nature.' (S.3.Q34)

Through these changes, we can also come back into synch with
our essential human nature. For humanity has strayed from this
balance with itself. We have, as Abe reminds us, 'been running
away from this truth for some time now, through fear of stagnation and no progression.' (S.3.Q34) We have been perpetuating
this falsity ourselves, albeit unknowingly.

We need to move more into open-hearted connection
by dropping our programmed conditioning. So much of the
time we are moving through life with our arms hanging by our
sides rather than with arms out in an embrace of life. This only
slows down our potential for advancement and moving forward
into genuine human evolvement. It is necessary that we permit
ourselves to move into the vibration of allowance and not give in
to the suppressive energies of others. We are not here for contain-
ment but for expansion. It is time to shake off the social identities
of separation and to shift out of these denser vibrational patterns.
If we did this, then external structures of division would no
longer be able to hold power over us. What is needed is to bring
the story back to ourselves: 'First, recognize your humanity. For
when you realize what you truly are, you are humbled.' (S.3.Q39)
The spirit of the cosmos literally flows through us. When this can
truly be acknowledged, then 'you will not be able to restrict your
being again.' Growth will then be inevitable, and this shall be a
step toward bringing a new world into being.

We should think of ourselves as a neuron within a planetary brain, and just as we can rewire our own human brain (think
of neuroplasticity) then likewise we can rewire the pathways of
our planetary mind-body. As Abe puts it: 'your individual brains
creating another unified brain being that of the planet - then of

being of the cosmos. The neural pathways are created by vibrational resonance, and so within is also that without.' (S.3.Q40) Can
we imagine this: a whole new set of pathways and connections
across the planet? This would entail a distinct new set of local and
global systems and structures. Could this be possible? We shall
never know if we don't first make the 'pathway change' within
our own brains/minds. Maybe this will begin from the work of
communities, re-envisioning how we live and work together. Yet
first we shall need to move out of our splintering and fragmentation. This too is a gradual step on the path of human evolvement:
'When you see that this way of living can only allow you to thrive,
then more and more will join in this new way of being. There
are such better ways to harvest your energy on this planet and
these communities will do so.' (S.3.Q41) And yet, to go forward
we shall first need to take a pause to realign and readjust. It is
then that we shall be able to step forth with aligned energies and
to radiate for others. No more will the essence of the human heart
be hidden: 'you have but hid yourselves away and gone within –
it is but time now to shine, quietly whispering to the ones whom
are lost, "I think I know a way out."' (S.3.Q42)

Can humanity find this way out? It seems so: yet it is not a
path for one person alone. What has been hidden must now come
forth to 'know itself' – the precious jewel that is our wholeness
must come to remembrance. From this realignment can come new
patterns of human interaction: 'we would like it to be seen that
you share and communicate and interact and but be in life with
the new skills and the new ways and ideas.' (S.3.Q43) This shift in
vibration and patterns – a re-wiring of the individual, collective,
and planetary body-mind – is not 'a shouting off the rooftops
or preaching but of a whisper to the ones who want but something else, something real.' (S.3.Q43) It is time to make these new
vibrational pathways, and for a different form of human-plane-

tary organism to emerge. If there is to be a momentary phase of detachment, it is for the reason of realignment and re-gathering. Humanity should not stay away from itself for too long. There is a future awaiting our participation; and that future also concerns our sciences and technology.

SECTION FOUR – Science & Technology

By the very nature of the Continuum, everything has always been and always will. Existence did not have one specific starting point – a 'Big Bang' – from where everything began. And so, the 'Big Bang' theory cannot be applied to the 'beginning of life' but it can be applied to the beginnings of physical manifestations – and of these there have been a multitude. Science has long been based on seeing things related to human time. Our dating of galaxies, planets, stars, and the universe itself, is given human-based timings. And yet time as we know it is a phenomenon relative to our perception of reality. It is not an Absolute. Neither are there 'pinpoints' of time where causes and effects can be measured with any accuracy. Rather, everything is vibration – and these vibrations are recorded by scientific instruments and given interpretation. Also, vibrations are interpreted according to the instrument doing the recording. We tend to think that the instruments we use – our mechanical inventions – are objective and deliver universal truths. And yet, such mechanical instruments are created based upon our perceptions of reality; thus, they too shall be an extension of this. The 'Big Bang' theory is a particular physical-material interpretation of events. Yet, within the larger vibrational picture, it is certainly incorrect. It is not that big bangs don't happen, it's just that existence doesn't work by starts and stops: 'it is not the beginning and there will never be a neat little packaged end for this timeline – that you do so hold onto in your physical existence is not so but a circle, a constant becoming.' (S.4.Q1)

It may be said that the universe that we inhabit is one of many similar, or not so similar, universes. And in this, such universes may have their cycles of duration. All these processes form a part of an ungraspable complexity of interconnecting life: 'It is one of connection, of interaction and, like you say, harmonious interrelationships of this one vibration, being transformed into worlds and living beings and stars and planets.' (S.4.Q2) An almost incalculable array of life manifests and goes through physical expression, all within a grand complexity of vibrational interrelation. It is, as Abe expressed earlier, a grand dance. And this dance is 'spread out experiencing all things across all created timelines and structures and languages.' This dance 'contains it all.' And this dance is of vibration; and 'this vibration was the beginning of it all.' (S.4.Q2) The physical body can feel and sense of this vibration, yet it can never contain it. Parts of this Source vibration can flow through the human body, and this allows for greater participation in what is also referred to as the *flow of life*. And quite literally, it is this. This Source vibration interacts, connects, and transforms the endless flux of the Continuum. Each life expression is a magnificent part of this Source vibration: 'it is all but one thing – one truth, one vibration, and you are it.' (S.4.Q2)

Everything interrelates. In this, what we refer to as multi-dimensions or multi-dimensional is just another term for *multi-vibrations*. A physical existence is placed within a specific vibrational pinpoint – our 'vibrational signature' – and so we are generally unable to experience these other vibrational realms.

However, all existence is within the 'sea of vibratory communication.' But if the human body could sense more of this vibratory sea, then it is likely that it would be 'over stimulated and burn out quickly.' This is why there is the process we know of as evolution: 'This is why evolution is key. It is a slowing down of what you already are – like a fine wine to be sipped and enjoyed and revelled in – to be fully immersed in the experience.' (S.4.Q3) A fine wine is not gulped down or swallowed whole in one mouthful. Likewise, vibrational pathways do not suddenly rush in or they would engulf, or overstimulate, us: 'But see this, it will not flood in; more so, a revealing of the pathway - so long as you can keep taking vibrational steps forward.' (S.4.Q4) Each step is revealed to us as and when we align ourselves with its resonance. Evolution is like an energetic attractor. At each stage we align, resonate, and shift into that new vibrational alignment or state. We are pulled along by the force within us that aligns and connects with a corresponding force without. The universe as we know it manifests from what the sciences call a quantum energy field. This quantum zero-state (to use scientific vocabulary) is the Continuum – it is also US. The energy of the Continuum is available to us as we evolve as human beings. As we develop our alignment, we allow more of this energy. And as we allow more of this energy, we evolve. It is a transactional relationship: 'You are able to harness this energy as you evolve, and you evolve by allowing this energy also. It is a transactional interaction, for the energy always has to be equal to the mechanism.' (S.4.Q6) If this process was not done in steps of alignment, then we would likely blow a fuse. The same also applies with the electrical power that is received into our homes. When it leaves its source – the power station – it first needs to be stepped-down through a series of transformers before it reaches the home. Otherwise, if it arrived in the same state that it left the power generator then it would blow all the appliances in the house – and most probably the house too. As Abe stated, the energy received needs to be aligned with the receiver (mechanism).

The quantum field, or zero-state, is often confused with a state of *no-thing* – hence, it is zero. Yet, somewhat ironically, it is the All-state from which manifests all known physicality. It is also a place of rest from where there is evolvement and return: 'it is a resting point at which all is ready to go again and again.' (S.4.Q7) Energy of the Continuum expands, interacts, and changes form continually. There is never a place where it is not. Everything has its state of rest between the dance: 'It is a waving, a peak and trough, a high and a low, around and about, and all this time a dance of polarities is really just the dance of one.' (S.4.Q7) We tend to perceive a difference between unity and form, as is form is somehow distinct from unity rather than being a specific expression of it. Something cannot be pulled out of thin air, out of emptiness. There is never emptiness: 'For you never just pull something from thin air but from an all-inclusive pool of consciousness. Call it quantum, call it ABE, call it you...' (S.4.Q8)

The closest that the sciences have come to what we may think of as 'emptiness' is dark energy. Current scientific understandings around this concept are still very sketchy and imprecise. Dark energy, Abe informs us, is 'a place at which things cannot be measured, for this is the zero-state.' (S.4.Q9) There are terms used for states that cannot be accurately measured. To give it a name creates a signifier, a marker of recognition, without having to understand the phenomenon in depth. Dark energy is still an enigma to our sciences. To name something is not the same as understanding it. And dark energy is not understood for it is the Continuum itself. The *Thing Itself* has not been seen. Instead, we have an assortment of words and terms. The cosmos is filled with life. Life is a continual expression of the Continuum. And yet, there are physical aspects within the Continuum which can be perceived and studied. Black holes are just one aspect that we can gain greater perception about within the cosmos. The cosmos functions in a similar way to the human brain. Just as neural pathways are developed in the brain to make vibratory connections; so too does the cosmos create pathways that connect at vibratory points (Black Holes). As Abe states: 'Black holes are but the connectors, the points at which when vibrationally aligned will open to reveal a connection, a joining up.' (S.4.Q12) Black Holes are like cosmic synapses, creating pathways to stars and aligning with them vibrationally: 'one giant brain, one giant consciousness.' When different neural pathways are developed within the brain, a new capacity of perception is created. The same also occurs for Black Holes. New vibrational pathways within the cosmos allow for an expansion of awareness within the cosmos. All are points of attraction. All is inter-relational. Human science tends to focus on forces of expansion and contraction within the cosmos rather than forces of resonance and vibration. All is frequency. To understand frequency and vibration is then a pathway of perception to grasp the 'interrelationship of things.' Vibrational connections are continually being made and remade.

The expression of consciousness is expanding through cosmic movements, within galaxies, solar systems, and their alignments. Galactic alignments too are pathways being 'carved out' and creating vibrational connections. These galactic and cosmic alignments then have vibrational effect upon evolutionary pathways: 'it creates a shift; and in that shift you then create a shift and then back and forth and around and around. You see, it is all communicating vibrationally, and always has.' (S.4.Q15) This is a vibratory conversation that has always been going on. And as Abe says, all we have to do is 'allow and listen.' In allowing this energy to flow forth, connections are made – expansion occurs that then allows more energy to flow. Those people who allow this energy to flow are enabled to make more vibrational connections that then allows more flow: 'in allowing this you enable it and when you enable it you allow it to manifest in physical form. You are making a necessary connection, and in this evolving.' (S.4.Q16) What we need to do is make a shift from material to cosmic frequency. By staying in 'material frequency' we are blocking the flow of cosmic frequency. As humans, we can allow cosmic resonance to flow into materiality – yet we are blocking this most of the time. We should also recognize that we are never apart from it: 'You are but blocking it out and shutting it down for you do not understand that part of yourselves; and some who do, have over-conceptualised and tied down something that so just wants to flow.' (S.4.Q17) We are being nudged to 'rhythm up, get in tune' and to listen more.

Without this synching up and getting in tune/resonance, humanity will keep itself apart from the rest of cosmic life. Although humanity is never separated, there is a dissonance that creates a vibrational distancing: 'It is not because you are separated at all; it is that there is a clouding – a mist, a fog, an engaged line or fault on the line would be a better term – that does not enable you to connect and receive.' (S.4.Q20) Just as new neural pathways are created in the brain, so too can new vibrational pathways be brought into existence. Everything aligns with resonance, and resonance allows new vibrational connections to form. As Abe says, discovering our vibrational essence is key for our shift in consciousness that will then create more pathways. It is a tightly interwoven matrix. Until humanity can develop more vibrational pathways, its exploration off-planet will always be limited. We need to discover ourselves more before we begin to venture out into the cosmic neighbourhood. As a species, we are not yet ready for moving away from Earth and exploring further afield. First, we need to develop our own connectivity within ourselves: 'we would see it be for this: to benefit the cosmos at all you would really as a whole species have connected more - united within and without.' (S.4.Q21) If we are not united within ourselves then we are only bringing more dissonance into the cosmic neighbourhood. Our first step is to 'discover all that you are and piece it back together.' Otherwise, our outward attempts at colonization will come from a 'splintered mind' and this will only hinder our way forward, not benefit it. If we are to move off-planet, then this momentous step should only be taken from a place of unification: 'This step, we feel, should always come from a place of unification for it to be of any use or benefit to your species.' (S.4.Q21)

To continue to evolve requires the frequency of increased unification. Dissonance is a de-evolutionary vibration; or rather, a stagnating frequency. It is harder to move forward when there is dissonance and imbalance. Any species intent on causing dissonance would be a less-evolved species. Dissonance is a sign of evolutionary immaturity. And for one aspect to evolve in frequency resonance, so too must another that is aligned with it. This is the situation for planet Earth. As the planet evolves, humanity will need to shift also, otherwise we shall not be in resonance: 'you have to take the jump at some point from a crumbling tower.' (S.4.Q23) The more we remain in dissonance, the tighter the restrictions will be. In a sense, we create our own little boxes of fear that then controls us. We need to piece ourselves back together, as Abe puts it. And part of this involves stripping away our conditioning. By stripping back, we can then create new connections that allow a shift to a more aligned frequency resonance: 'Your circles will get larger and expansion will come naturally. But it will only ever be from this place of unification.' (S.4.Q24)

Technologies and the Human Being

The future pathway with technology is a complex issue at this present time of humanity's evolvement. How we go forward now as a species will determine the future development of and interaction with our technologies. To some degree it seems inevitable that technology will merge further with humans. This is already happening in terms of implants and devices that assist in our health (seeing, hearing, walking, etc). Yet this merger, or combination, between technology and biology should arise within a natural flow – from 'these unforced pathways of evolutionary connection.' As always, it depends very much on the place where we are coming from. Are we coming into technology from a place of unification or from a splintered mind? As Abe states: 'know all that you are for if you can really grasp this as a whole species it will surely be a quantum leap for you in evolutionary terms.' (S.4.Q25) If the human being is splintered then there is a lack of wholeness, and therefore clarity, in all that comes forth from this. The state we are each in is then mirrored in the things we do, and which manifest from our actions and thoughts. Abe gives the analogy of baking a cake; if we only had part of the ingredients then we could not bake a complete cake: 'You see, there is great intention of making the cake but if you do not have the complete ingredients to make it then you may well end up with something that was not intentional at all.' (S.4.Q26) We each need to be grounded, and this is increasingly important in a world that still remains splintered.

Technologies in human use are advancing and developing at an incredibly rapid pace. This is bringing the human vs. machine debate to a peak point, and we cannot delay for much longer in coming to an understanding on this matter. At present, humanity is developing technologies not from a place of unification. As such, we are placing ourselves out of synch with these technologies and their use and influence over us. Abe is very clear on this point:

> But we see that the way in which you are going is not from a place of unification – of knowing of this vibrational essence to everything. You really cannot delay this any longer for your species is on the cusp of moving forward. This is why we have continued to manifest, to say "hold on – let's get this part right first and then when we truly understand this, then we can move forward." (S.4.Q27)

We truly need to understand ourselves better before venturing further down the road of technological advancement for we have arrived at a crucial stage along that path. We cannot remain asleep at the wheel as the juggernaut of humanity races into an uncertain future. If there is dissonance within, then surely this will manifest without. Similarly, if there is balance and harmony within us, then this too will radiate outwards in all that we do. We do not need to be perfect before moving forward, although we at least need to be more united: 'We are not saying you should be a perfect species, for there is no such ideal, but to know truly and understand truly without a doubt that in which you are.' (S.4.Q28)

Technological advancements are a part of any civilization's evolvement, whether on this planet or others. Everything is a part of the evolutionary journey through the cosmos and within the Continuum. Technologies are those resources that we use for our interaction within physical reality. We should be growing alongside them – not to be under their control and manipulation. As Abe states: 'Controlling and manipulation will always try to push forth. In some sense, it is in the knowing of what you are is where your power really lies.' (S.4.Q29) What is important here is that humankind, as a whole, finds its own grounding and unity, especially now as artificial intelligence (AI) has emerged upon the scene. Yet, as we know, the 'controlling and manipulation' will try to push forth on this matter also. And this is the case, as much of the funding, research, and resources around AI comes from people and groups in power. From this energetic space, it is likely that AI will be utilized for further consolidating of these pre-existing power bases. In other words, those who have an interest in the status quo will use AI as a means of strengthening the incumbent status quo. As Abe says, they are in it 'for the race.' The issue here though is one of power. People have been conditioned to believe that the many are under the power of the few: 'you always think that you are powered by such people when in reality it is the other way around. The masses are awakening to this dissonance - they are claiming back their power.' (S.4.Q30) AI can be an enhancement for human life, if it is used from a place of balance, harmony, and unity. As in all cases, when a tool falls into the wrong hands then the consequences can be unpredictable or even harmful. There is little doubt at this stage that human evolvement will include technologies and a path of technological advancement. This road itself may be rocky for a while: 'We are by no means saying that this transition to unification will be a complete easy ride, for there will be destruction and dismantling of old structures.' (S.4.Q30) Yet the old must make way for new connections, and this may also involve a certain degree of discomfort for a time.

Part of this discomfort will come from questions concerning what it means to be human. The quest for meaning, to put it simply, will push forth yet again. One of the features of existing within a physical realm is that we naturally assume that 'meaning' is something that can be found outside of us: 'It is never outside of you. You have been conditioned in such a way that this is always sought outside of yourselves, but it is not so.' (S.4.Q31) Meaning is something different for each person. It is what each of us makes it to be for us. Meaning can also come through our connections, and this can be separate from living in a controlled social environment. Perhaps we are all trying to know ourselves through ourselves; and in this, we only need to truly *be* ourselves. It is when humanity stands splintered that it becomes powerless. This is where, and how, the control manipulations come into play – through humanity's divisions. Power is only really a game from the few. It is always the few who are greedy for power, for it is not an inherent human trait. Technologies in the hands of the few is like anything in the hands of the few – it will serve their agenda. Yet there needs to be a harmonization in this. Physical existence is a polarity; and in this we need to find a balance: 'bringing back to balance is key - centering yourselves first.' (S.4.Q32) Everything is about balance, for there are many impacts and influences that can quite literally re-wire our brains. In this context, virtual or augmented reality spaces and video gaming are two such examples. As in everything, discernment and perception are required; so that we can know the difference between what a fake environment is, what is not, and when we are 'in play:' 'for the ones that are of entrapment are really the ones stuck in a reality and are unaware that they are but playing a game at all.' (S.4.Q33)

Technological advancement should be about enhancing life and not diminishing it. Any technology that creates dissonance and disharmony is not in alignment with humanity's evolvement: 'be very wary if a technological advancement creates dissonance rather than connection, for this will only be moving you away further from the truth, enabling the few to keep this power and redeeming you as powerless.' (S.4.Q34) We need to be wise to this situation, and for awareness to spread out amongst humanity. The more people who are aware of the dissonant use and manipulation of technology, the more it can be 'taken back.' Technology, when in resonance and alignment, can allow humanity to explore itself, the world around us, and the cosmos of which we are a living part. And in this expansion, we shall also be 'creating greater and greater neural pathways within and without in the cosmos.' The way ahead, Abe informs us, is by 'promoting connection and pathways' and thus moving further away from our isolationism. In moving forward, we should be mindful to stay within natural processes and not to get too caught up in the possibility of technology to steer humanity away from its biological potentials. The human body-mind is aligned with a vibrational environment and opening up to new resonant frequencies will in itself trigger evolvement and change. We do not need to try to force this by technical interventions, especially when coming from a place of fragmentation rather than unity. There will be, for example, those people wanting to extend life through technology; yet this may interfere with natural rhythms and vibrational shifts. We need to grasp the whole picture, and to recognize that we are not only separated, physical bodies: 'we understand that you would very much like to prolong your experience in physical form. But we also see the need not to meddle in it too much, for you will upset the natural rhythm if pushed too far and that could be catastrophic. For not only you but to that of the whole cosmos.' (S.4.Q35) There is a fine line, we are informed, between enhancing and 'completely dominating, controlling, and forcing life' for all existence is relational and one effect may vibrationally alter others. Life is a 'balancing act' and the way forward for humanity is through being 'much more balanced, much more smarter and much more in flow, trying not to cause further dissonance.' (S.4.Q35)

Balance is also about stepping back when it is necessary to do so, and not trying to impose ourselves too much. Humans have a tendency to force issues without fully grasping the implications of the situation. How can we impose balance when we are not fully sure what or how balance operates? As Abe reminds us: 'balance can look destructive and chaotic like things are far from balance for your social constructs have built their buildings upon changeable foundations.' (S.4.Q36) Fluidity and change may not appear to us as a process of balance when in fact they are. We cannot be sure when events may take a different course, nor the reason for such sudden changes. We need to remind ourselves from time to time that we are not in control; rather, we are in the flow: 'life has this funny way of changing direction within a heartbeat – come back to yourself, feel back into your bodies.' (S.4.Q36) There is a time for doing and a time for being. We should gather ourselves back in before rushing to step forth – and this is our *way back home*. We should not be attached in racing ahead, for all our racing is only done from straight lines. Humanity still overwhelmingly perceives in linear timeframes, and linear routes. We are less inclined to sense in cycles, in the eternal here: 'there is nowhere to get to so long as you can see that and not be attached to future or longing for past. That you are merely here with life and able to do these wondrous things within this time-space reality.' (S.4.Q37) We are in a state of becoming and that is not constrained by linear timeframe thinking. The interaction of existence is the core; and time throughout the cosmos is experienced differently. Existence is 'the one constant and infinite becoming.'

Another pathway of technology relates to energy extraction/ creation and usage. For a long time now, our 'developed' civilizations have been too dependent upon primitive, and highly controlled, sources of energy. There has been a shift to less physical energy sources such as electricity and nuclear power. Yet these are still, in the grander scheme of things, primitive forms of energy. The great step into understanding how to utilize the energy of the Continuum – the zero-state field – will be when we shift into a greater understanding of vibration and unification:

> There is infinite power in this source of zero state. But you see, you can harness this for yourselves for this too is of you and from the world around. No longer will you have to rely upon physical material sources to power your world, but to look to vibrational attraction for this is the key that holds much power. (S.4.Q38)

However, Abe warns us here that we first need to come to our place of unification before we are able to utilize this 'infinite power' – otherwise, 'this power could be used for destruction rather than benefiting yourselves as a species.' The next step is for our human sciences to gain further understanding around the functioning of vibrations.

Slowly – ever so slowly – our sciences have been shifting from the visible and measurable into the realms of the non-visible and unmeasurable. Yet there is still too much emphasis upon existence as separate, atomistic parts: 'When science can see the vibrational element is really no differing from that of your physical existence it will go much further.' (S.4.Q39) Matter and vibration needs to be aligned for they are not separate but are aspects of the same phenomenon. This merger could also be regarded as between matter and spirit, for spirit is vibrational consciousness. In this merger could come great discoveries and leaps forward in human evolution. This misunderstanding between spirit and matter is what Abe calls 'merely a fault on the line, a contamination of sorts.' And when this blockage is finally passed, then 'it will be of fast movement forwards. Of infinite expansion of mind, a more cosmic communicative system.' (S.4.Q39) As the human brain creates new pathways within, so too will this create new pathways of connection and communication within the cosmos – everything is interrelated. There is so much out there within the grander cosmos that is waiting for humanity. We have just not arrived yet – we have not yet *arrived to ourselves*. Humanity is still largely expressing itself from a collective splintered mind. And an 'allowance of vibration' can never flow into a splintered mind. Without this expansion into the greater flow, such advancement into the cosmos will not occur. The vibration of unification must first be understood and then for us to shift into this frequency resonance. As Abe says, it 'is in the knowing of when to put it aside and to be of service to yourself, and in this to the whole.' (S.4.Q40)

The splintered mind still thinks in boxes and in separate categories. By exploring the cosmos from this mindset, we will be developing more tin boxes with fuel propulsion. We are thinking in terms of material apparatus for exploring rather than in terms of expanded consciousness. The splintered mind thinks materially; the whole mind perceives beyond the material and into the consciousness field. Vibrational alignment can, and does, exist beyond the body. Perhaps there is way to travel within the cosmos that is through the consciousness and without having to take the body along with us: 'the more pathways that are created through you, and then within the cosmos, the less need there will be to explore in a physical sense for you will see that consciousness is but free to travel and is not as constrained as you once thought so.' (S.4.Q41) We can thus envision the cosmos as being a brain with multiple pathways and connections. There is no coincidence that many explorers of consciousness have referred to their experiences as being within the 'cosmic mind.' Some recent commentators have suggested that reality is similar to a computer program. By that account, we can also say that reality is a cosmic mind, and it is all within the 'one thing:' 'if there is just one thing and you are it, then what is within is also without on a larger scale.' (S.4.Q42) There is endless communication happening within the cosmos, even if we are not aware of it. Everything is in an endless conversation – the cosmos is in communication with itself. The cosmos is also in conversation with humanity, with each one of us, only that we mostly do not 'hear' or perceive these communications. We haven't yet picked up the phoneline.

We, as untold billions of individuals, need to pick up the phoneline for ourselves. If we do not do this, then power over us will continue to be centralized into the hands of the few. And these few hands will continue to develop technologies that support and strengthen their consolidation of power. And this shifting will be uncomfortable for us: 'it will be a struggle for you have allowed it for such a long time and have left many things dormant and gathering dust. It is not a battle of power as such; more so, a shift.' (S.4.Q44) Humanity, as a species, needs to regather its pieces back together again. A new vibrational field resonance needs to be created. It will be this resonant field frequency that will force a shifting of social structures: 'the more and more people that are understanding and knowing of this unification, this vibration in which you are being shifted to resonate with, to understand, the more these structures will not be able to withhold.' (S.4.Q44) Evolution is vibrational, and those species that cannot move into the new vibration – resonate to the new systems – will become extinct. Abe is quite clear on this point: 'the animals that became extinct were the ones that could not resonate to their systems; and therefore, could not continue into the new vibrational evolution.' (S.4.Q44) To move forward, to evolve, humanity needs to step away from its layers of social conditioning and to allow for a greater connection to an expanded consciousness field. That is, more consciousness needs to flow through humanity, through our vibrational signature, and into the physical world. We are the conduit for this resonant energy shift. This will then trigger new faculties of perception and cognition within the human species. Humanity needs to regather by first having a good clear out: 'One could liken it to a good clear-out of such, then put back once you have given the shelving a good dusting.' (S.4.Q45)

The human being can be the place of power – and not our mechanized structures. Manipulation occurs when the few have control of these mechanized systems that we then submit ourselves to. Within these mechanized structures we become further splintered and kept in psychological separation. By allowing more flow of consciousness, we then create more pathways both within and without, and this can bring forth new energetic arrangements with a shift in resonance. Splintered minds will use technologies for selfish means; whole minds will seek for collective evolvement. The more that we focus on material aspects, the narrower our perception becomes: 'the more and more focused it becomes the more it is pinpointed, the more splintered your existence becomes. Open up and you will see the greatest power source and in this you will discover yourselves.' (S.4.Q47) Our splintered focus is taking away the discovery of ourselves. We place our focus and our power onto physical points-of-place. In this, we need to make a readjustment – a realignment. We have been contaminating our own pathways of communication. We have restricted our thinking by seeing the physical human being as a limitation: 'you have been contaminated with the notion that you are a physical being and even though this is so there is much more to you than that.' (S.4.Q49) It is time that we allowed 'new forms, new pathways, new ways of communication.' We also have to evolve in resonance with the planet. We have to adapt to new ways of being: 'when your planet shifts you have no other choice but to shift with it and this goes further and further...' (S.4.Q51) And at the core of everything is pure consciousness. This is the Continuum – pure consciousness.

Evolution is all about taking new pathways at appropriate times. And when required, some pathways need to be dropped in order to move forward. We see the taking of new forms all the time in Nature – from the cocoon of the caterpillar-to-butterfly as well as the seed being cracked open into a new form of life. New forms are what continually take us forward and help us evolve. And these new forms require resonant, coherent vibrations – not splintered, fragmented ones. Splintered vibrations allow for weaker manifestations in physical reality. A coherent resonance brings more power: 'unification in oneself is much more a powerful force in the world than a splintered vibration.' (S.4.Q54) This is why Abe says that we need to strip ourselves away – to take it back 'to the bare bones.' We need to take our heavy layers away so that we can regather and bring ourselves back together: 'in this unseen non-physical part of existence, is the key to many leaps forward as a species.' (S.4.Q55) The unseen world has to be in harmony with its physical counterpart. It is also a true gift to be in physical form, as Abe reminds us. These communications are here to benefit each one of us, and to allow us our own pathways of development and expansion: 'Our true purpose is to hand it all back - all the constraints that have been put upon you by others and all those that you have put upon yourselves.' (S.4.Q56) The *Way Back Home* is through ourselves, as we peel away our own self-imposed restrictions and step forth with greater clarity and faith in humanity.

SECTION FIVE - Humanity & its Future

W e are at a pivotal time for humanity. It is necessary that we evolve forward and do not stagnate. It is time now for many people to step away from their boxes of separation that are the result of social conditioning. Many people's 'vibrational signatures' – i.e., the vibrations that represent their physical point-of-place – need to open up to allow for a greater flow of consciousness. Many of us have been conditioned into social personas and to be the 'good citizen' and yet we are losing touch with a core vibration: 'your consciousness is like the glue that will piece what you really are back together again if you so allowed it.' (S.5.Q1) So many of us are living our lives at less than full capacity – we can achieve so much more. Yet in order to *breakthrough* to a new level of existence, we first need to experience a *breakdown*:

> you can only have a breakthrough if you have a breakdown of old paradigms; and if old is crumbling then it paves way for new pathways, new connections, and in this breakdown there will be great breakthrough as people will be searching within themselves for some-

thing that resonates; something that sticks; something that makes them so feel human again. (S.5.Q1)

We need those triggers that will compel us to seek for a new resonance – to 'feel human again.' Humanity needs to shift forward through a series of vibrational nudges, as if we are moving up a ladder, one step at a time. In recent years the quantum sciences have discovered more about the unified field (the quantum field) and how vibrational fields operate. This has been useful in helping humanity to grasp more of the bigger picture, the larger energetic cosmos, of which it is a part. Yet at the same time, there has been a tendency to view this unified field as something mystical, or as belonging to a special kind of transcendence. In short, we are doing what we have always done – to frame it, name it and claim it. But this is not something we need to reach higher to. Everything is here now where we already are. And where we are within this unity is also expressed through polarities: 'The only way to unity is accepting the light and the dark, the love and the hate, as but the same thing because within this unity you realize that you are perfectly imperfect, and that is wonderful.' (S.5.Q2)

There are many triggers and shifts that humanity is going to experience in the years ahead – much is changing. It is a time for uprooting: uprooting from the past in order to move into a different future energy. This will take time, and yet it will feel as if it is an accelerating, snowball experience as so much will be happening in these years: 'for people will feel a gaping hole where what once stood a statue of self, and you had built your whole world around it.' (S.5.Q2) Many of our old patterns will be uprooted, and in these spaces, these gaps, will come new pathways and connections, and new flows of consciousness. We should not be in such a rush to fill in these spaces with new boxes of content. We need to allow us to breathe again, for 'life to flow uninstructed' through our very being. So many attachments need to be stripped away from us so we can step forth in a lighter way. All naming and claiming will need to be dropped – including the claims we have placed over ourselves. The important thing is that we can participate in our future. The pathways that can be taken are fluid, and so the outcome can be more aligned if we are consciously aware of our participation. There are sets of potentials, and these potentials contain their own fluidity. We are here to navigate these pathways. Humans are dreamers – yet are we conscious dreamers? Humans are so conditioned to be active and doing, and wanting to force ourselves upon situations, that we have almost forgotten how to *allow* through our being. We need to find the balance once again between awareness and allowing: 'You are aware and also allowing - this is resonance of your very being. This is resonance to your planet, and this is resonance to the universe.' (S.5.Q4)

Humans have grown up being conditioned to laws. There is a law for everything, and a law to explain everything. Our science laws are taught to us in school. Social and cultural laws are given to us by parents, government, and institutions of authority. We think everything can be explained, categorized, defined, or given order. And we have become dependent upon many of these structures for they bring a sense of regulation, order, and balance into our lives. Yet in the process, we have lost touch with the creative spontaneity of connecting and trusting with flow. All is a vibrational resonance. And we should be within resonance; for when life is out of resonance, there is disruption, imbalance, and potential breakdowns: 'You have long forgotten your vibrational essence and how it is tying and binding itself to things and places and people and experiences, and future outcomes and past problems. One simple thing; one thing – vibration.' (S.5.Q5) If we can remember vibrational resonance then we can remember ourselves. All physical manifestation comes from a source of vibrational resonance. All forms of interaction have a basis of resonance. We would do well to be consciously aware of this. One of the obstacles here is that many so-called 'New Age' or pop-spirituality teachings have talked about vibration in an abstract way. We have been told many times to 'raise our vibration' – yet what does this truly mean? We have been given the sense that we need to reach somewhere – to transcend, go higher, go out of ourselves, etc. When in actuality, the opposite is required: we need to come back to ourselves. We need to strip away all the layering and baggage that we have placed over/upon ourselves: 'Give life room to move again within you, for there isn't a state to get to - it is here. It's just that you have the blinkers on, the social blinkers - take those off and allow all that you are.' (S.5.Q6) Vibrational resonance is not a 'state to get to' but rather a *beingness* that is within us. We need to be in resonance with the world around us, but not be imposing ourselves upon it or by forcing new laws upon a natural world. The resonance is to be achieved by creating new pathways and connections of inter-relationality.

We each act as transmitters of resonance. When we are in resonance then this ripples through the vibrational frequency field. The Continuum is a vibrational matrix. Yet resonance should not be forced: 'it is of not forcing at all but of you continuously resonating at that at which you are - and in this it will break through at some point, weathering away at that contamination.' (S.5.Q7) Resonance is like rain against stone – it will gradually reshape the physical form over time and exposure. At the same time, it is important that our own resonance is not contaminated by others. This is one of the dangers of being exposed to over-stimulation both through the online world as well as in our social environments. A person should be grounded – balanced and in resonance – before actively attempting to influence others. And again, this is often the weakness of many people who set themselves up as 'teachers' of others. Each of us needs to come from a balanced state of 'home resonance.' Our modern lives are so full of hurry and haste. We have been conditioned to hurry things up and just get on with it. We are told that its good for life to be predictable and known – to be familiar. Yet, in this way we have also become increasingly disconnected from a source of meaning in our lives: 'For a splintered mind creates just that - a splintered world, and in that a splintered cosmos.' (S.5.Q8) We have come to believe in so many things – in the *this* and the *that* – without realizing that all the time *we are it*: 'In this realization that we are it, in this deep knowing that "oh yes, it's all the same and I am it too," you let up the character.' (S.5.Q8) There is so much conditioning that we need to unravel ourselves from. We are continually in a process of becoming.

Because our current programming is one of resistance to anything that is not physical, we shut ourselves off from allowing vibrational resonance. We have become restrictive to our own allowance, and in this we constrain ourselves – we block the flow of consciousness. We need to step back from this self-constraint and to rest and regather. We have been conditioned to shut out the possibility of communicating with the field of pure consciousness. The Continuum sounds to many people like a hollow shell when this could not be further from the truth. The Continuum is a dance of conversation – of interaction, connection, communication – a dance of life. Most people have lost the ability to listen: 'you have been conditioned in such a way as to shut this out, for it is not of service, to keep order and obedience.' (S.5.Q9) If we can truly allow, then we have the potential to allow pure consciousness to be expressed in physical form. This is the merging of spirit and matter. And this is not only for a few but for everyone: 'This is not available to just the few but to each and every one, if they do so allow. Drop it all and allow.' (S.5.Q9) This is the future pathway for humanity – to move into conscious communication with the pure consciousness of the Continuum. By loosening our vibrational constraints, we are allowing more of the expanded energy-resonance to flow through us. Some people may feel anxious at this point, feeling that they are going to lose themselves – their ego or sense of self. Yet we shall not be losing what we always are: 'in the allowance of the new vibration it shakes loose the contamination that has been considered your vibrational signature for so long.' (S.5.Q10) We shall only be losing our contamination, our layering; our vibrational essence will be harmonizing with the vibrational resonance of pure consciousness. So that we can move forward, we first need to pause, to rest, and regather ourselves. We can then 'move forward again from a different place.'

This moment of regathering is necessary as humanity has become out-of-synch with its vibrational alignment. Technology has created some of this dissonance, although not all. And over the years, humanity has been given nudges to assist its re-alignment. But now, something stronger is required: 'you have not been inclined to feel that nudge. Now, it has to be more so of a blow rather than a nudge.' (S.5.Q11) As a species we are not yet sufficiently unified, or connected, to be making the best use from technology. We can see this clearly from the behaviour we witness online and in social media. We are still too splintered for our technologies to be of most use to us. As mentioned before, this is a danger for it can create much dissonance and dysfunctional consequences. Humanity needs to respond to this situation, but by awareness and vibrational re-alignment, and not by taking itself further away from life: 'it is never about ridding life of yourselves: sitting upon a hilltop void of self, void of world, no.' (S.5.Q11) What we need is to strip it all away – to strip back our socially constructed false self. We need to allow the expansive vibrational essence to flow through us: 'allow this vibrational essence to flow through your being, birthing a new vibrational signature - a non-splintered one, a unified one.' (S.5.Q11) Humanity needs to take off its bandages and to allow its wounds to heal. It is time to shift into a more harmonized species vibration; this is crucial now. A more aligned and vibrationally resonant humanity can emerge from this – 'one consciousness at a time, one vibrational alignment at a time.' And this is where human beings can be of purpose, both physically in their everyday lives and also in alignment with the resonance of pure consciousness.

Human life is also about the expanding of our field of consciousness; to allow pure consciousness to manifest through the physical human being. The physical being is biologically encased, yet this does not mean that we should be encased in our limitations of consciousness. Humanity has already explored far and wide. We have gone deep into our oceans, far across the Earth, and high up into the atmosphere and into orbit. Yet if we don't explore and reach ourselves first, then we shall have found nothing: 'You can only ever but find yourselves. But if so coming from a splintered mind, you are finding everything else but yourselves.' (S.5.Q14) It is time to open up the closed; to reveal the unrevealed. How can we be going towards the "post-human" if we have not yet arrived at the *fully human*? From becoming more ourselves, new pathways shall open up for us – a new resonance shall be gained. A new sight shall be revealed: 'they will be new to the eyes that have not yet been open but old news to those that have been awake.' (S.5.Q15) The human is both within *being* and *becoming* – between stillness and movement. This is the flow of evolution and has always been so. Consciousness has always been in flow through humanity, yet it manifests in relation to the pathways that have been created. That is why it is now time for new pathways, so that pure consciousness can flow more abundantly. It is time now for a recalibration: 'To harmonize what is available to you at your next evolutionary step of creating vibrational pathways - not only within but without too.' (S.5.Q17) By recalibrating our human resonance we are also rewiring our internal pathways – not only within the brain but also within the DNA: 'DNA is receiving this new shift, this new alignment. All is in conversation - it just depends upon what conversation it is, and what you are so to allow.' (S.5.Q18) As Abe says, it all depends on which conversations we allow; and from this, we recalibrate (or rewire) ourselves accordingly.

By recalibrating, re-wiring, ourselves then we are also dropping old patterns (patterning) and habits. As connections and patterns are internally shifted, so too will this affect our outer lives. To shift the outer, we must first shift the inner: 'opening up for new pathways to be formed which are more of resonation to your being and to that of which is trying to manifest in form.' (S.5.Q19) Outer forms are energetically (vibrationally) attracted to align with inner resonant frequencies. This is why inner unity, rather than fragmentation, is crucial now. We cannot hope to establish a harmonious outer civilization if its people are splintered within. Our human future will always be in relation to our inner state – in relation to our degree of unity/harmony or fragmentation/dissonance. For so long, the human path has been one of a restriction of consciousness. Now it is time for a change, a readjustment; time for a little nudge, so to speak. Abe refers to this using the analogy of a child riding a bike: 'Take, for example, a child riding a bike - you gently direct and readjust for the child can take this or leave it. It is completely up to them and in this it creates the paths.' (S.5.Q21) The critical question now is whether we allow ourselves a nudge into creative pathways of evolvement; or whether we let ourselves be steered into a dead-end street. We can know what the better pathways for us are by feeling into the aligned resonance. It is not a question of hunting for obscure secrets, like some adventurous Indiana Jones, but rather of aligning with our home resonance: 'in this you realize that there was never a secret to be found - you just had to allow yourself to fall back into resonance into you.' (S.5.Q21) By allowing resonance, we are also allowing the flows – the rise and fall of the waves – and knowing when are the moments for rest and regathering, and when are the moments for action and stepping forth. By struggling against this ebb and flow we are creating a flat-line: 'to fuss and fight and to have to constantly keep it in a straight line of resonance you are in hindsight flat-lining life. It is a constant balance between the two, and to know when is where you have to re-attune yourselves.' (S.5.Q22) Like a musical instrument that has not been played correctly for a long time, we are in need of a re-tuning. Otherwise, we shall not be permitted to rejoin the grander orchestra. As Abe reminds us, life is not about picking sides; rather, life 'is a wave of vibrational potential.'

As a wave of vibrational potential, we should also recognize that such waves, as mentioned, have higher moments and lower moments (vibrationally speaking, and not relating to position or merit). And it seems that at this current time, humanity is experiencing a period of lower vibrational resonance: 'you are but in a dip. It is the time to readjust, realign, and then move forth. For if not so, you will continue with this path of resistance and constant action.' (S.5.Q23) This is our moment for regathering and recalibration. It is the time for a readjustment and return to humanity's home resonance. Abe refers to this as *The Way Back Home*. We are told that in constantly struggling by way of action, we are actually flat-lining life: 'You are straightening it out, and also it goes for the other end of constant rest. It has to be of resonance - of movement, of rest, of breath.' (S.5.Q23) The energy is always there, available for us, only that it needs to be in resonance to the 'mechanism or organism that is receiving such vibrations.' And right now, the human organism requires some recalibration so that more expanded energy, consciousness, and awareness, can come forth through us. It can be said that humanity is in need right now of this 'nudge' so that we can align with the necessary vibrational frequencies. Once this readjustment is made, greater flows of consciousness can be merged with; a connection to 'cosmic consciousness' can be made. Yet these connections need to be of resonance: 'The connections cannot and will not be made until your own individual pathways have been readjusted, reset, and reunited.' (S.5.Q24) And by the Abe communications coming forth at this time, they are part of this 'nudge.' And humanity is also a part of that nudge too.

For many a long time, humanity has intuitively felt cut-off from its greater cosmic inheritance. And now we know why. We have needed to realize, or be brought to awareness of this situation, this turning-point: 'At some point you need to stop - gather and rest, readjust, and realign with this wave, this vibration.' (S.5.Q25) Until now we have been like the lone singer in a choir that has been out-of-tune with the rest; either singing too fast to race ahead or singing too slow and being left behind. After all, vibrational resonance is a dance – but it must be a mutual dance. And this dance must be made up from participating individuals. Yet first, we need to strip ourselves back 'to the bare bones of things' for there has been too much contamination. A new signal must come forth from the noise. It will not come immediately from the whole human species, but a rebalancing needs to begin – and has already begun: 'it will be this way and more and more will follow. Like the cycle we talk of, you're stepping into a dip, whereas the old action orientated resonance is too much - it is going around again to rebalance.' (S.5.Q26) We shall either become exhausted of the old ways, the old patterns, or we shall be forced to leave them behind. Either way, there is little future for humanity if we remain within the old vibratory patterns for they are now of stagnation. We are now within the period of rethinking our choices. This is the readjustment period; and there shall be some discomfort: 'It will be one of discomfort, for all readjustment is uncomfortable. For if you have been sitting in a certain position for a while, when you come to move to another position it is of discomfort, is it not?' (S.5.Q27) And the degree of this discomfort will depend upon how strongly we remain attached to our old patterns and paradigms, or how willing we are to shift to a new pattern-resonance. The next decade especially will be critical for deciding upon humanity's future pathways. And although it is always difficult to predict timelines, it shall be dependent upon our behaviour – as individuals, in groups, and collectively. This shall be our tug-of-war moment: 'it will be a tug-of-war between what is and what wants to become. And could even see this time shortened, so long as people can recalibrate.' (S.5.Q28)

The information that has been communicated here is 'of importance now,' according to Abe (to which I would agree). As a species, we are in tremendous times. And we are seeing the fragmentation and splintering all around us – not only locally but across the globe. We are in need of a species unification that respects our individual and cultural diversities: 'People are the key connection, are the source, and unification is really what you are.' (S.5.Q30) We come forth into life expression and return to Source. This is the cycle of life. And when we can understand this then, as Abe says: 'you could probably loosen up a little and allow all that you are to flow through you, unrestricted by what you have been conditioned to think, to be.' (S.5.Q30) I feel it is fitting to leave the last word to Abe – to the pure consciousness of the Continuum of which we are all a part. We are a part of this great wonder and not apart from it. It is time to come home to ourselves – to find *The Way Back Home*:

The time is now to understand your extraordinary existence and at the same time your very ordinary existence - this is true unification of being. And you will see that you start to breathe again, you start to live again, and you start to love again. What a journey. You see, in this you realize you have come but full circle - but this time you are awake, you are alive. With much Love and Light - ABE. (S.5.Q30)

PART TWO:

THE ABE COMMUNICATIONS

SECTION ONE - Setting the Scene

1. Hello ABE. Can you explain 'who' is ABE?

We came forth as a collective of energetic form, but we very much understand that form is not classed in which your worldly physical reality is, so let us explain. I am ABE, I speak for many for in this plane of existence separation is not of essence. We are a multitude of which is not ever born into the world of physical form as you know it but understand we are very much still a part. Take it like this - you are experiencing the world in your physical form in that you have a body; this body is not separate from the whole. You are of a denser vibration in which resonates to that of your home in which you are a part of. You are in physical form which means that you are energy like us but stood still as a point of attraction; you are part of what is all motion, ever-changing but you are stagnant just for a short time. What we are, and I cannot come up with anything else that will enable us to speak of an individual consciousness for it does not exist here and it will not exist for you when this time is over. What we are is what you are and life is never apart just taking form moving through and out of form, like a candle that burns down to liquid because it has changed its physical form - does it really mean that the candle is all gone? I am able to be an 'I' for the essence of communication; to be able to come forth in such a way that will enable us to convey that which is important. That your life here is of beauty and difference and separation but here it is of collectiveness and oneness, free from conception. What we want to come forth to do is unify the two essences together to enable a humanity of divine essence, of divine being, to realise that in which you are and that in which you can become. We want to guide you to the way back home, here and now. Love and Light - ABE

2. How would you describe your location in terms of place or space?

See, we are able to have space and time and place because of you. Like an antenna that picks up radio waves they are never positionally located until a device is enabling it to be transformed. Our point of place is here at this moment but not of location at all. What is enabling us to come through is that the mind is expanding as you evolve. This will be so as to let in more and more. What we want to do too is to enable this transition - to know of it but to also help guide so that it will not be of confusion. As to what is happening, we feel that at this time there is an epidemic as people are struggling. You see, like we say you are stagnant, and you cling to this in your form. Energy is shifting you along and coming in to help flow but like a dog with a bone you will not let go. Love and Light – ABE.

3. Do you experience time? Does the concept of time have meaning for you?

Time is not a place, a point, it is really a social construct. It will never be able to be rid of as this is your human structure. From the very first part of human activity you have tried to ensure and predict and prove that I am here, and time says so. This is really the essence of time - to locate and divide and direct one thing; to slice it up into little sections. But if you think right now you will see that time is false for when can you ever trace back? It is only memory and it is so that it is happening right here and that too of your future. Knowledge that this is so then enables you to use time as it is and not how your existence has taught it to be. Love and Light - ABE

4. Would you describe yourselves as a collective consciousness that perceives as a unity? Does this mean you gain experience collectively?

Yes - we are a collective consciousness. A web of consciousness, one could say, in which through all of time and space and place; experience is woven in inter-relational, interconnected, and picked up as to what you are attuned to.

For you have your eco-systems right down to the very energy at source - your bodily eco-system, your environmental eco-system, and the cosmic eco-system all different levels, perceptions, points of place working in perfect harmony at each and every level but non-separated at all. Our connection would be that knowledge of what you are is lost. Our connection is to enable you to see this interconnection, this vastness of perceptual experience; that there is a wholeness in this separation and that which looks like discourse at one level is harmony at another. Love and Light - ABE

Let us come forth as to what true knowledge is. Philosophers all throughout time have depicted and try to understand what knowledge is. True knowledge from our standpoint is allowing that in which you are. All knowledge is knowable, it is just that you think that it has to be attained - every experience, everything, every flap of a wing, crush of a rock, birth of a child, cry of a death, are all a vibration, a part of a pattern intrinsically interwoven into a web of consciousness. All is known, everything that we know is what you know. There is no separation in this; this is really what we want to come forth to do. Take, for example, technology; it has allowed you to communicate all over the world. What you have within you is much more expansive. Each and every one is a part of this cosmic consciousness. It really is so; it is just that life has caused so many to be fixated on the known physical essence of your being and forgotten that pool of consciousness that is readily available to each and every one. When you understand this then you have knowledge. It was always there, our only advantage point to you is that we do not have the dense energy in which you call body. Love and Light – ABE.

5. How can people develop their understanding of these vibrational levels and their harmony?

You ask about the levels in which the harmony works between each and all levels. Put it like this, it is vibrationally inter-relational like the body with its environment. Although they are not apart from it, it correlates, it speaks vibrationally to one another. You have just found this out through the study of trees and its communicational pathways. Everything is talking to one another whether known or not. When unknown your vibrational essence can be hard and cruel acting upon all that is around. Even if you do not utter a word, one could say that this web is an ever-expanding web of consciousness created by vibrational essence. Harmony is only sought between these seemingly polarities when all are connected, for if the heart was cut off from the body it would not function. As so with the whole of life -communication is of essence and with correct knowledge of what that actually means is of essence. We are not to say that it should be acted upon. No, quite the contrary - harmony is not something sought out, but something allowed and opened up to. Love and Light - ABE

Our feelings towards humanity is always one of great love for how can you not love part of that in which you are for that would defeat all that we are? We are not here to say that we are above and beyond like many would like to be thought of, but we are a part of that in which you are and in which everything is. We want to show you this; to be open to the beauty of contraction and expansion. With Love and Light – ABE.

6. Has any part of the ABE collective had experience of the physical realm of existence?

Yes, all have. Like we say, this field, this pool of collectiveness is forever dipping in and out of form. Religion tries very hard to describe this as Karma. Karma would be action, like there was something that acted. But what we say is a constant becoming; we are not of body; we are not of what your mind may conceive us to be. Therefore, it is very hard to put in words this consciousness is of one but also of many. Love and Light – ABE.

7. Can you elaborate upon what types of physical existence has been experienced by the ABE collective? On this planet we call home and/or other planets?

Understanding of these levels is about vibrational alignment. To that of which you want to understand you can only ever move to that of the mechanism, the brain. To understand would be to evolve but to evolve you must first understand that you are so much more than your physical essence. That is but the starting point. For energy to experience physicality it has to have a point of attraction. This point of attraction is but the construction of the mechanism through time things have evolved. Every planet is different; every planet is vibrationally aligned with that in which it harbours. Like we say, it is inter-relational. If you are asking if there are different life forms on different planets, then we would be inclined to say that it is abundant all over the cosmos; but is a vibrational match - that is why you cannot see it. It is not recognizable in your form to be able to see. But as you evolve you will too see that the whole cosmos is alive. Love and Light – ABE.

All of life, all forms, for we can only say this because we have no form; to have no form is to be all forms and although we construct ourselves as a collective we are a collective of all consciousness - all times, all space. This is the fundamental key that all you are and what you will ever be comes back to this. You may not have Nicola or Kingsley as you do so now but there will be an impression of that for you too in this form or should we say as none for there will always be an essence of you. You are but the same. Love and Light – ABE.

8. Is there a part of the essence or consciousness of Nicola and Kingsley within the ABE collective?

But of course. There is no separation at all. It is so inadvertently intertwined we are surprised that there is even a construct that could perceive separation at all.

It is all about vibrational alignment. But see this, we are zero-point now. You see, all over the cosmos life is evolving at different rates. We are not here to hurry your species along in any way shape or form but to assist in the energies that are being felt. We have been to Earth many times before and have been mistaken for aliens or spirit, but we are neither. We are what you are evolving to but also that in which you also came from. Now to answer that in which we communicate to others we only do so to assist, never to direct, but to broaden the scope. As to the stage of what the species are at, there are always people that are susceptible to subtle energies, although some are very much constricted to their physical life but some are not and it is easy to convey with such ones. As for the word intelligence, we would say that it is really been over humanised for intelligence is the way in which you collaborate and harmonise with your environment. It really is not something to gain but to be relational to. Therefore, if that is so the case, then it would be relevant to say that we communicate on all that can vibrationally align. This is done so by allowing flow without the stagnant self in human form, but not so in all other forms as this is not an issue. Nicola is vibrationally aligned because that signature in which you hold onto all day long is dropped. One could say that it is a falling into rather than a trying to align to. Love and Light – ABE.

9. When you use the term 'vibrational signature' are you referring to the human mind/personality – or self – that gives the vibration a particular manifestation?

It is so. It is like the paper filter - a dissolvable one, but when it is no longer in resonance with the body becomes whole again. But hear this, your laughs, your smiles, and love resonate within others. With much Love and Light – ABE.

10. You said that ABE has been to Earth many times before and have been mistaken for aliens or spirit. How did this occur if ABE is a zero-state field – did a part of ABE manifest in form?

It was never as the form of ABE, you see, but of a filtering of consciousness of which the organism is resonating at. You see, it is allowed through you and will inspire and come forth in such a way, even if somewhat constricted by the brains conditioning. Is this of understanding? You see, this is but more unlimited in a way we have been able to come through previously and this is because of evolution of the brain and the neural pathways. But see this, when there are so many pathways it will come back to but one. With Love and Light – ABE.

11. Is our evolution somehow linked together? That is, we need to harmonize our energies so if there is disruption here on Earth it will affect the evolution of the other planets?

The whole cosmos is interrelated and harmony within this system is of importance, but it is not led in the way you think and destruction to you may seem like harmony to others for your planet is always morphing to the energies available. See that human conditioning is so to be seen of doing and acting and although there is need for this there is also a time to be guided by that. Many people are resonating below that of what the planet is resonating at and therefore out of harmony. Then there are others who are resonating highly but maybe are not of the world. For your own evolution it would be wise to marry the earthly energies to be in sync with that first and foremost and to connect also with the cosmic consciousness. This is your evolution-ary path at present. This would then harmonise the planet and that of the cosmos too.

12. Are there other species not of the Earth who are here in physicality in order to resonate highly to assist evolution on this planet?

No, it is but a calling of this one thing. You see, it may have been necessary before because you were not developed enough so would have come through a secondary source. But now there is no need for this as you are evolving. Is this of understanding now?

The reason you can dip into this cosmic consciousness is because you are very much a part of it but when in physical form you are entitled to block this out completely like changing the channel. You cannot hold and hear two stations at the same time, but in the future with your bodies changing to receive more and more energies then this would be possible of other species. Remember, this where we are coming from is a place of zero-state; also, your body is limited to the energies it can receive which is a good thing. At present for to go from one state to another without progression would be detrimental. It cannot be that way. ABE.

13. You state that our present evolutionary path is to connect with the earthly energies. How can we best achieve this?

Yes, it is very much so needed to be able to align yourselves to this. Firstly, many have lost touch with their environment and like the lizard whose receptor was covered up in an experiment you are lost and out of sync with your environment and when this is so, you are not functioning well. You are sick, out of balance, for to take the environment away from any species you see that their health deteriorates. So, it is of utmost importance to start resonating again to your home vibration. This is done so by that inter-connectedness, of being in nature and of bringing nature back into the system. It seems that in your earthly existence things have become very much sterile and although may be seen as good has wiped important things out that allows this relationship between home and self. Realise this - there is never a separation and what has been taught is that there is so, and in this creating a great dissonance - correlation not segregation. ABE.

14. You also state that we are morphing to the energies available. Is this how evolution occurs on this planet - by adjusting to shifting available energies? If so, what is the origin of these energies? Many people feel we are currently experiencing a transition upon this planet - is this connected to a shift in 'available' energies? Can you explain? Thank you.

The energies are available from all around the cosmos. The original state is the zero-state: the zero-state is this endless becoming of form and of no form. Life is cyclic. Evolution is very much a vibrational process but also a material one too. See it like this, a human is physical in time and space; vibration is not only felt it is transformed to that of the environment. It is so very tightly interwoven that it is hard to see a starting point within your physical existence. It is correlation and transference that allows evolution in physical form, but it is very dependent upon the energies available to it. See a toaster - the toaster is working all well and good when the mechanism is capable of transferring the available energy to be of use to something within the environment. Higher energy for the mechanism will blow the fuse and be of no good; too little and it will also not be in sync to do what it has to do. Do you see? There is a transition and like we say it has to be a process rather than a jump. To get to the home resonance is important but the next step is evolving to be more holistic. In that being the cosmos, we understand that it is very much in action as we see such energy rooted in so many. But even so the social construct in which you are within is making it difficult to enable these things to flourish and we realise there will always be a struggle to create the new. But it is turning, and it is a process. Like we say, we are not here to spread dire news but for people who are not exposed to this kind of information to see and connect to something that has long been forgotten and is engrained in the wholeness of your being. ABE.

Energies, vibration, is always available to those who are open to it. These energies are also from this state of zero, manifested into physical form because of resonance. Some people can indeed tune into other vibrations that are seemingly not present to that of the masses. See, it is their own vibrational signature that determines the syncing up of vibration. A relativity of such for relativity in the sense is a vibration syncing up or a system, a mechanism, that is able to receive such a vibration - one could say, more universal. ABE.

15. You state the importance of connecting and being in balance with Nature. Yet our governments are pushing toward further urbanization and persuading people to live in cities. Isn't this contrary to the direction we need to go in? Could this be a deliberate policy to create further disharmony upon the planet?

Of course, this is so. Maybe not so intentional although we understand some is; but lost in the ways in which have been deep rooted for so long. People and not just governments do not want to lose control never understanding that they never once had it anyway. What is damaging to your home is only damaging to oneself and most people are just not harmonised at all in this de-harmonisation - you can do nothing but spread that too. ABE.

16. You state that we are at a time where we need to be guided. Are there other intelligences guiding our evolution upon this planet or working to assist us? Could you explain more on this? Thank you.

We are happy to be connecting today. We would like to communicate firstly that yes, we are in touch with other intelligences but see it like this, we are also not separated from them either. You are very much at a young stage in evolution compared to others, so we would say that we are not communicative with so many of your species. With other species around the cosmos this is not so as they know that indeed this separation from what we are and what they are is not definitive in no way shape or form, and in this we don't come forth in the same way as what we would to you. See, life is very singular, and we come forth to you in individual form or collectiveness to communicate and get across that in which you really do know. Sometimes you need to just wake up and remember that is our purpose. ABE.

17. Is there a reason why you are communicating with us?

The reason is that you will bring these messages forth in a way that haven't been before. Your hearts are very much aligned and opened for this receiving. Not many are so in this way. In your non-egotistical open heartedness, you can receive and that is what is happening here, a clear channel, a clear heart. ABE.

The reason to communicate with you is because of again resonance. What we also would like to say is that the time is right, and people are all evolving at different rates for that is the beauty of life in all its colours and diversity. What we would also like to say is that indeed we do communicate with others but see it like this - if you are aware of this kind of thing as we know that others have come before as to convey messages of love and light you will understand that the message is loud and clear and consistent and that is of unity, of collective collaboration; maybe not in body form but of a singular consciousness, one source. There are levels of consciousness; see it like this, to be that of a Russian doll; the further in you get the smaller and smaller the space. This is so with consciousness. ABE.

18. So, you communicate to other intelligences - including ourselves - through vibrational alignment? Would you refer to this as a form of thought transference, or telepathy? Is this the fundamental form of communication in the cosmos?

Ahh telepathy, a heightened subject within your realm of existence. It is but the communication of the cosmos. But see this, it is not something that you are anticipating; no, but something in which you are to allow to open up to. See, this form of communication is not something that you are making your way to but to a way in which to remember as to that in which you have always held. You have long shut out things in which are part of your being of this world. You have many distractions and things to keep the mind occupied and stimulated but you are yet to understand the magnetic vibrational alignment form the core, the heart. Vibrational alignment is and always has been an open heart, for when this is closed off, you are not able to fully communicate. You have long been lost in language. I remind you of the saying, a good old heart-to-heart. This is, it opens; this is resonance, this is truth. ABE.

19. You say that the way of communication of the cosmos is a way we need to remember. This suggests we have fallen into a collective state of forgetfulness, or detachment? How can we move back into a state of alignment or resonance?

Yes, your planet is but in a slumber of sorts. The way to move back into alignment is to connect with each other, with the planet, with oneself. See, it has come about that relationships are dire in all aspects of life; with your beautiful home; with yourselves. There is nothing but judgement and condemning of feelings and emotions, like it is unnatural to feel and that one should toughen-up and get on with it; make something of yourself, and the relationships to each other to be that of competition. Not many show their true selves, their true feelings, through fear of the heart being broken. That they must defend it at all costs; but it is not true. The more open your heart is the more authentic your life is, and the easy life can move through you; and in this not being continually offended by others. ABE.

20. Do you have any relationship or attitude toward our species, humanity?

For isn't all just one relationship? We will say that again we are not separate so for us not to feel deeply for your species and that of your planet would be shutting a part out of which we are - then who would we be to be allowed to speak of unity if we are so splintered too? Our position is that of unified consciousness and although it seems to be that we are from another realm and something apart, this is really not so. The relationship we have is unity and for guidance from us to be able to receive comes from your own splintered mind, it is not of our separation but of yours. When this is so you see yourselves as acting upon the world or the world acting upon you. It is not - it is a collaboration of consciousness filtered down through smaller and smaller, tighter and tighter, constructs. To see the wholeness is to really be in collaboration and to be in collaboration is to be in harmony. ABE.

21. You suggest that we should 'open our hearts' and be more trusting in our emotions. Yet we live at a time of great emotional manipulation and exploitation, especially through our media. Is there a danger of becoming emotionally unstable or vulnerable if we move into our heart space?

For wouldn't it be the best time to do so when such things look so dire? Yes, people give you reason to not trust, but in the very closing down of your heart space do you not then close off to all that you are and all that you are to be? For one to be open-hearted could be said to be one of a selfish act, for you are the one that will feel life openly & honestly, therefore experiencing it in a way that is meant to be. We are not saying that you should be passive at all; an open heart is guiding and if you truly are open then you will receive much more from life. Is it not that what it is all about? ABE.

22. Since there is no separation between us, as you suggest, then in communicating with ABE humanity is actually in conversation with another aspect of itself? Is this the same as being in contact with our 'higher selves' as told in mystic traditions?

You see, the higher self has too been very much conceptualised, and even though it is an aspect of you it has been taught to be a place to aspire to in most traditions. That this higher self is meant to be of highness as suggested in the name but is not as so. One could say an aspect of that in which you are but also an aspect to that of which we are. In communication with ABE you are indeed in communication with self. We like this very much; we want you to understand that there is so much division in your realm and we use realm lightly and match this up to the analogy of the Russian doll as we would not want you to misinterpret that there is some place OTHER. ABE.

23. Have you communicated with Earth or humanity on previous occasions? Have we known you by a different name in the past?

We are always in communication with the whole of the cosmos; it is just dependable upon what is open to receive, and at what the mechanism can allow. See it like this, we have conveyed with other beings, they have conveyed with your planet through others that are open to their guidance. It is an interwoven inter-connecting vibrational web of communication. ABE.

All the knowledge of the cosmos is available like a symphony, an inter-weaving of existence. Our relationship is but the same as your relationship in that it is an interaction of seemingly opposites in a world of unity. For to discover anything of your planet, like greats who have come forth and dove into this pool of knowledge before, it has to be interpreted into form. These greats of humanity did but one thing and they tapped into this, into us; they stopped trying and just allowed. You see it as when you write - if you are thinking how to do so your writing can become entangled. To truly write is to allow what wants to come forth at this present tense. ABE.

24. Is the ABE collective synonymous with Source? Has humanity in the past had contact with ABE and interpreted this as God?

Yes, is the only answer we can convey here. It was of a time of very much a singular polarity mindset in which was captured and overtaken for mass suppression of that in which you are. We feel that it should not be interpreted as God or source as these words are but too much over-used and overburdened and really get in the way of that in which is truth. ABE.

25. It may be difficult for some people to accept that the origin of life, and of religion - the Source of everything - is a zero-state field. We might get a few blank faces! Would ABE like to comment?

There will be people who are not of resonance to this, of course, and who may stare at you with a very much blank expression. But hear this, as the pathways are built in those who are of resonance they are making the vibrational connections; then the pathways will start to be built too in physical form and in physical form people will see and in this will allow these to be built internally. Is this of understanding now?

26. How would you prefer to express this concept we have as God or Source?

We would like to convey it as unity or unification to be a better word - the unification of self. Too long you have been splintered and divided. This is how things are now seen in your physical realities and have caused great pain to the masses, not only on your planet but to that of the whole cosmos. ABE.

27. How has this caused 'great pain' to the whole of the cosmos - could you please clarify?

Of the de-harmonisation and destruction waving out as a ripple throughout all of time and space.

28. Is this why there has been much activity to communicate with humanity in order for us as a species to find re-alignment and resonance?

Yes. We are here to guide and for you to see the unity in your existence and to connect you back up to that in which has be long lost. ABE.

We would also like to add that although there are cosmic repercussions from such disconnection it really needs to start at the base and that is unification to one's self. There can never be anything universally accomplished from a splintered mind. ABE.

29. There are wisdom traditions that teach a 'spiritual science' - a path of inner development - that may include certain exercises and visualizations. How does this path correlate with what ABE is saying about connecting with the unity field?

We would like to say that it does not quite correlate in a way - that a different approach is needed now. For so much has been contaminated, like a Chinese whisper that has gone around the world far too many times and now does not correlate at all to the original words first spoken. You see, it has gotten lost in translation. But hear this, you see there are not some long drawn out notions of healing within a person; it is simply coming back, a coming back to this. You see, it is but so simple that you overlook it for you think it must be drawn out for all this contamination took but so long to accumulate. But it is not so - it is an almost unity 'oh yes' and you can see and keep picking yourself up and simply bring it all back in. Is this of understanding? You see, we do not want to say that these traditions have not been of use and could possibly help someone loosen the grip in which you hold so tightly to your splintered self. But see this, you make it as easy or hard - it is but your choice. ABE.

30. In the past there have been communications with other 'collective intelligences.' Can you comment on these communications? Were they expressions of self that were intermediaries, transmitting information from Unity?

All is but an expression of this, yes. It is but one and if you were to collect this information all in one place you would see that it very much interlinks with one another. The reason in which we have come forth and have continued to do so is to take it back to the bare bones, if you will. Your species are evolving; no doubt it is seen across your planet, people waking up from the suppressed states. You see, it has been an infection of mind in that it has been too overused the way bearers will be the ones who keep their hearts open when all others want to close them off and put them under lock and key. ABE.

31. You say you have come forth. Should we interpret this to mean you have become more manifest at this time in order to assist in our understanding? Does this imply we are at a significant moment in our planetary evolution?

That is exactly as so. And this is why things can sound in contradiction, but they are really not. For something to come to form it has to be of no form first and foremost.

32. Are there currently other minds on this planet receiving direct communication from ABE?

Not in this form, no; and not of present time.

33. Why was the name 'ABE' chosen - for any significance?

ABE is significant as to what Nicola brought forth of her own being. Like we say, it is of collaboration; this was a fitting name to that of which you would say abbreviation in that we can be of contraction. Is this of understanding?

ABE was short for abbreviation: abbreviation meaning a term that is of something that is of contraction; shortened, lessened, meaning we are to put nothing into one thing as to shorten, to put a doll inside another doll.

34. You said that you have never been born into physical form, and yet you also state that your 'collectiveness is forever dipping in and out of form'. To us this sounds like a contradiction – could you clarify what you mean here?

Ahh good morning, a good question in which to start with. The contradiction you see is of course from your own standpoint and we see it as so that there is no separation. For whatever is form, we are of it - but we would never take the form as ABE or of any of the collectiveness. We are not a form - like we say, more so a pinpoint - a point of attraction than a form. So, we have never been into form, but our formlessness allows to be in all form but not of it. Is this understandable?

35. Understandably, from a human standpoint this is a difficult concept. If there are ways to clarify further, we would appreciate this. So, would a part of ABE dip into physical form, such as part of a species? Is this how universal manifestation operates?

We would like to use the analogy of the ocean and the wave, but we see that this too has been used by many. We would not be in physical form for we are specifically a point of attraction of which is being channelled.

Never of form but you see what we are and what you are is not any different, so I am in form but not of this form. We are eager to answer these questions, and we thank you for your continued connection. We do feel so that this communication can move on quickly now. ABE

36. By being in material, or dense form, is life in service to the unified zero-state? What can be understood by the concept of 'service'?

We would not like it to be one of service, for you see you would be putting yourselves in a form of hierarchy of consciousness. It is but differing stages and differing views. You see, if there was one big crash of a drum and that was that, it would be but an awful waste for you wouldn't have time to dance for the moment you would of stood, the song would of been but finished. Is this of understanding?

37. There is a phrase we like. It says – 'Simplicity is more complicated than it looks.' The truth of our connection to Unity is simple, yet we have complicated these matters. What would ABE say to this?

Like just discussed, the constriction of self is always up to you. You can resist and hold tight to that of which you know and feel comfortable with to continue - or you can allow much more. Is this of understanding? You see, simple is always hard for you in human form. For you see that if it is simple and comes easy then it is of no importance. You know that this is not true at all, for life should flow. You clearly need to participate in this life but life does not have to be battled with, just met. ABE.

38. For millennia, humanity has talked about spirituality and the spirit. We have long searched for spiritual understanding. Is spirituality as simple as connection to the unity zero-field and allowing pure consciousness?

We would like you to see not as but a connection in a sense that you have to get up, plug in, and be of doing - but rather an allowance of. For if you are having to connect up in some sense, then you have simply lost the notion of it all together. It is but an allowance of it - to breathe, settle down, and allow. Is this of understanding of how spirituality is? For we would like to say that you are already spiritual, for you have just forgotten about your vibratory essence and connection to all. It is really a remembrance. It is but an understanding of what your heart already feels and picks up. Do you see? ABE.

39. So, the big question (and we have to ask it!) - what 'is' the meaning of life? What are we here for?

For the whole meaning of life is to live, and to live one must be allowing of all that you are. For to not understand that you are but of physical content but also of vibrational too, you are but living a half-hearted existence. But we think you have gotten the notion of this, so we will put it like so: meaning of life is *you*. There is no particular meaning that all of life should abide by. But hear this, meaning in life does so get lost when one is very splintered for it feels like the whole world has taken a piece of you and you are but lost within the noise outside of yourselves. You see, we would not want to wipe the whole world clean, void of expression, for the meaning of life - if it is to be of anything - is this EXPRESSION of but one thing. For you see, there would never be a dance of life if one had to do it all alone. ABE.

SECTION TWO - Mind, Body & Spirit

1. We often use the term 'God', yet this is misleading. What is your understanding of 'Divine Source'?

Ahh yes God, the word that has caused so much hatred in your world when all was to be seen was the complete opposite. You see, we have come forth for this reason; because we do so indeed see that like we said, things need to be stripped back to the bare bones and this is so with your understanding of the divine and also of God. People are of course free to choose in that of which they do wish so but for the ones who are not drawn to any of these terms, and we do so feel there to be many now, we want to say that God, Divine, universe, source, are all but one thing – and you are it. ABE.

2. Have earthly religions been successful in representing the Unification/Source?

We see that they have, and we are not saying that they have not served a purpose at a different stage of your evolution. What we are saying is that to move forward now these outdated ideas are not going to serve you well to see the whole picture. They are not so much to be rid of or dismissed, you would not say to your mother 'oh well, you gave birth to me a long time ago, you are of no use now,' for we are in a large cycle in which some point you will come back to the beginning and this will be the forever becoming. There is truth in all religion, but it seems that these things are driving humanity in the complete opposite direction to that of which it was intended to do so. This source or collective or God is that in which you are - how could it be any other? You have been sleeping and it is time to wake up to that in which you are, which everything is. We know that a lot of new age movements are saying that we are all one and this is true unification, but we feel that they miss it out that this is also science; it is also God; it is also every terminology that could be ever thought of. You can never dismiss others, and people will always have their own beliefs - but what we want you to see, to truly see, and not just that but feel - in the core essence of your being - that even in this world of great polarity, I see you in me and me so in that. ABE.

3. To return to Source - is this what you mean by the way back home? Could you clarify what you mean by this term?

The way back home is really first and foremost back to the home vibration being your planet, and to be aligned with that for we feel it to be too much of a step to go from low to resonating high with the planet. This step cannot be skipped; what we also say is that to do so you have to unify. Within a split consciousness of 'me and the world' is never going to be able to see to it that you are a transactional vibratory essence that is not separated from your world - more so, an expression of it. This is not to say that you do not impress upon the world either, for you alter vibration by that at which you resonate - so it is always transactional. So, to be unified it would be to see and wholeheartedly feel that you are transactional, that you are whole. ABE.

4. How would you regard humanity's current spiritual state? Has our species had higher knowledge previously that was lost to us?

There have always been stages at which your species have been higher developed spiritually, but still it has been tainted by something outside of yourselves, that being of a God. The state of your own planet's spiritual evolution is progressing rapidly and has been so. That is why you see more and more destruction because of the fighting to keep the old. What we would like to say that there does not have to be a choice; just a knowing; a wholehearted feeling that what we are stating is truth - not because we say it to be but that you feel it deep in the core of you and resonates with you on all levels. ABE.

5. You have said previously that the state of our own planet's spiritual evolution is progressing rapidly. Does that imply that the planet is a conscious organism? Is the Earth also in communication with ABE? Could you clarify this?

Good morning both. We are delighted to clarify but a few things, and feel it is of importance to do so. You see, it is so; but one could say that also the Earth and all differing planets are of a constricted consciousness. By that, of its own vibrational signature and to that that is upon it and also around it. You see, like we say about the pathways - within and also it is also so without. You have your connectors within the brain that create neural pathways due to vibrational resonance and this is so with your Earth. Now hear this, as your planet evolves and morphs and changes it will resonate differently and like your internal self will also create differing pathways too. Is this of understanding now?

6. There have been many 'wisdom traditions' operating upon this planet. Did they have access to Source, to the Truth? Did you have direct contact with any of them?

Like we say, it would not of been of the ABE form; but we do believe that people have had this connection even unknowingly so. For some people, they are inclined to have this type of brain functioning in which they never lose this connection albeit how hard they try to shut it out throughout their lives. And there are others whom through evolutionary processes seem to have developed a masking of this connection and the brain develops differently. But this is not to be said that it is not available to them. One could compare it to, say, more so of a deeper sleep. ABE.

7. There have been many spiritual Masters upon our planet. Were these ordinary people who gained access to the Unification energy, or a deliberate material manifestation of consciousness?

But of course, we would like to tell you that all who have ever walked your planet have had this connection to unification energy. But also, too, it would be a deliberate material manifestation of consciousness because it would have come forth in such a way as this. ABE.

8. Are there other terms that have been used/are in use that may help to clarify the ABE state?

The one who has come closest would be that of Zen tradition; and we understand that you have to name things in your world of polarities. Zen too in a way has become tainted for it is seen as people taking themselves apart from the world which it is not, but this is now tied to the word Zen and people see it that they would have to give up all that they love. The only way is to be of it and in it; there is no truth up on the hilltops but here in the midst of it all, in the polarities of existence, knowing that it is all quite ordinary but seemingly extraordinary all at the same time. ABE.

9. Is true science a knowledge of vibration? If so, will we arrive at this knowledge?

We feel that indeed science is a knowledge of this vibration. But it can never be truth in the sense they can measure and record with seemingly pinpoint accuracy. But it is always going to have to compare things and always have polarity. In this you will find marvellous ways to be in your world; advancements and knowledge of it. We are never to dismiss this for it is who you are too. You are human beings of your world, but it will have to always measure and dice and slice and in that will not have the full picture. What we see though would be something of a merging. If science can see the completeness and the undivided essence of life within their boxing things up, truly see it - and we are sure it is already going in such a way - then that would be of essence. ABE.

10. Is vibration at the core of our health? How can we heal ourselves with the knowledge of vibration?

Vibration is a core essence of health care, for vibration is the language of life. For you to be out of vibrational alignment of your very own being, if you are split, then you are creating discourse within the body. Everything has a vibrational signature, so it is true with that in which you put into your body for that is what tells the body what the outside world is like - if it is thriving or not. So, it has to be of great importance that you are 1. aware of the vibrations of the things you put into your body and 2. that of your own vibrational signature. You see, this too is inter-relational. You could have all the best food and eat well and exercise but if your own vibrational essence is that of lack that you are eating this nutritious food, then you are no better off than eating all the junk in the world. For you see, there are people who are extremely fit in the world and have health problems because they are not aligned with their own vibration and that in which they are putting into their bodies. Is this of understanding?

11. Is certain healing knowledge being deliberately withheld from us? If so, why is this?

I think it would be of both. See it like this, there are people on your planet who know of these things and are keeping them alive within their communities. Indigenous people pass this down through the ages by ways of ritual. What has been done, that more so in the west, life has been pushed in such a way that this knowledge is seen as new age or mystical, that logical reasoning and science can be the only way. What we would like to say is that there is also a dissonance in this and if unified with the so-called mystical and that of science then medication will be a thing of the past. But you see, your very system has been built on such grounds now and will be difficult to re-establish without a fight of someone wanting to hold on to some sort of past. You see, it is never about one better than the other but about the merging of both - the unification in things. ABE.

12. What will be the future of human health? Will our health systems be forced to change?

The future of health really does lie in the people's way of change for they too need to shift and let go of past habits that do not serve them. You see, you know in yourselves and your bodies when something is off if you are attuned to your being, and you would know how to nurture your body back to equilibrium. But we are not saying that you need to be dismissing that which is of your physical world and science, reason and logic, for they are intertwined aspects of who you are and how you experience life as a human being. It is in the emergence of both that the key to health really lies, but we feel that both sides will find it hard to let go of their deep-seated beliefs at first. But it will happen. ABE.

13. What will be the future evolution of the human body?

The future evolution of the body will not be of the body but be that more so on the consciousness level. Not so much on the physical to start with but as the consciousness of your being rises, or one should say resonates, the body has to adjust too to the higher vibration in which way the body will not be so dense; it will not be so heavy. ABE.

14. Is this evolution of the body to a lighter form a natural evolution that occurs in all dense matter as it develops? Has this bodily evolution occurred before on this planet? On other planets?

It is a natural progression for they would not be in resonance. But see this, for you to become and be of this world there has to be some kind of density that is also resonance to that of your home Earth. This would be subject to all species and you will then see that really you do resonate on a physical level. It can be no other way. See, what we have now is what many people speak of as the love vibration that being of the cosmos and this is true in a way. We want you to see that there is an expansion coming, evolutionary, that will enable your species to expand in consciousness to that in which we are. But hear this, it will always be of a density to match that of your planet. It can be no other way, and this is so with others. ABE.

15. As the human body becomes less dense to resonate with an altered consciousness, then

how will this relate to the physicality of the planet and other species upon it? Will there be a similar shift in their density too?

Yes, it will. But see this, they will be subtle changes overtime and never a leap as you see it has always been so, and will always be, of harmonisation to all that is, of the planet too. Is this of understanding? It is always inter-relational, and you will not be of such lightness or transparency with that of your planet Earth for it is rather dense in its vibrational essence, albeit shifting. ABE.

16. How do you mean we 'will not be of such lightness or transparency with that of your planet Earth for it is rather dense' - will humans not be 'of the earth' in this time, or that the Earth will not shift in the same way as human bodies?

No, you will but shift to that of the planet for you cannot outgrow it at present. For the purpose of conscious evolution at this time is to put deep roots into your planet. Is this of understanding? But hear this, for if the planet is making other connections and is not at all of resonance to that of its beings, then they will grow increasingly uncomfortable upon it. Do you see this?

17. What is the importance of food and diet for human health and awareness? Can you say

something about the current state of our food systems?

It is important in the way that it is inter-relational to that of your own vibration. Like a sock in the wash that is dominant in colour it will colour all that is mingled within it. So, it is important. Like we say, it allows the body to sense what the outside world is like - a vibrational communication system. The current state is that it has been far way taken from its own harmonious balance to that of the Earth. To see that your Earth is suffering is to see that you yourselves are also suffering. You are creating a dissonance of vibrational communication through the toxins and chemicals that are being used at present and, in this, creating a cognitive dissonance. ABE.

18. Does a contaminated vibrational signature affect the food we eat and vice versa?

Always it does - it is but transactional. See it like this, someone who but knows no other than being that of their own vibrational signature are quite dominant in a sense to get their point across. Someone who may be not so caught up in it are not so and are seen as introverted or shy. But hear this, they are but allowing – see, it has been the dominant that has been cheered on for so long but in this you have gotten too caught up in this game. And we may have strayed again; but you see, the dominant force lords it over and therefore whatever is not allowing to meet and be of benefit to

135

the system is not going to be one of health or of nourishment. Is this of understanding?

19. What is consciousness? How does this function with the human body/mind?

Consciousness is the signature of form but also that in which it comes from. It is this. See this again with the analogy of the Russian dolls - there is consciousness, then there is the doll. This is form. Then there is another doll - another form. And inside that, another doll, until you come back around and there is consciousness again - space emptiness, one could say. Although space nor emptiness is ever void. You see, consciousness is always at a point of attraction to that of the mechanism, or should I say organism. To be pure consciousness is to be void of form completely. See, we have no form; therefore, we can be everywhere within all form but not of it. This is hard for your brain to conceive for it is always working within the parameters of polarity. It is about the essence, the knowing of this form and allowing consciousness to have a more fluid flow. Is this understandable?

We would also like to add that mind is not consciousness - it is your unique vibrational essence

20. Our histories, our experiences, etc – do these help to develop each particular aspect of consciousness? When each vibrational essence, or

consciousness, returns to no-form (ABE) does it retain any sense of individuality within the collective?

This is but a fine line. See it like this, a toaster which has the electricity running through it but when thrown away or broken beyond repair it is unplugged. You see, there is no obvious notion that it left or imprinted the electricity upon this one thing. But hear this, like we have mentioned before, it is a joining up for the evolution is not of just you, no, but that of the whole cosmos. To answer more direct, there is not a specific part of you that is in the shape of you. But you see, there is but a web of consciousness - to be one of connection not of form at all. But you see, it is a vibrational pattern that can be tapped into, almost like a membrane. Is this of understanding? But please, do hear this - it is never of two separate things, just a filtering through as such. ABE.

21. Our minds – or vibrational signature – also reflects our personalities. Could you clarify the relationship between consciousness and our individual selves?

It is but a filter in a sense. But see this, it is not two distinct things - but we do so feel that we have to explain as such. In your world of polarity, it is but always in and of itself despite the separateness you do so feel at times. It is a change of vibration in which to bring into form that of which you resonate of. Is this of understanding now?

22. How is consciousness linked to evolution upon our planet and within the human species?

Consciousness is what we are. See, we are only a point of attraction; because of the brain this then creates the vibrational signature you see as mind. Mind is not a part of consciousness; it is a part of that which is body. It is the unseen signature, your vibrational signature, that speaks in vibrational terms and resonates. Consciousness is devoid of form - it is zero point. Mind is not consciousness but your vibrational language back to consciousness. Is this understandable?

When mind is dropped, when you do not cling to that of your vibrational signature or self, pure consciousness is allowed to flow.

23. So human ego is blocking the flow of pure consciousness? Does this suggest that we should detach from our personalities in order to allow connection with pure consciousness?

You can never but detach - it's about meeting in the middle. In the knowing of it as unification, never a one or the other. But hear this, it may be of a good notion to but put it down and see - to rest without trying to uphold it as you do. ABE.

24. And how would this flow of consciousness be linked to human evolution? Is it also somehow linked to the evolution of this planet? That is, can we participate consciously with our planet's evolution?

Yes, that is so. In the allowing of consciousness to flow you are allowing life to move. We know you hear this now as more of a Buddhist view but what we want to say is that consciousness should flow, yes, but you should also be able to unite matter with this. This is where your evolutionary key is - there is no way at all that this energy will not be influenced in some vibrational way in your existence. It cannot be so, this is life, but in the allowance of it, it will really propel you forward as a species. Realise this though, we do not want any species to be void for what would be the point of that? ABE.

25. How would you suggest for humans to develop their minds? Are there any specific practices, such as meditation?

Mediation is great but sometimes can get caught up with escaping here to be in your body. To be feeling all this to be a part of all there is and also to be able to know the expansive truth too whilst here in physical matter – wow, what an experience. What a life. Be with it, feel it from the centre of your being, and most importantly – participate. ABE.

26. It is said that the human being has an organ of perception that can be further developed. Some traditions say this is necessary for our evolution as a species. Can you comment on this?

This is to be so of the pineal gland. There was an experiment a while ago which I think we may of mentioned previously, about a reptile that had this sensory organ connected to perception covered up and struggled to read it's environment. What we would like to say is that it had been of importance in a way. See it as this, you are a blind man of the world and you realise that driving may be off of the agenda. You still are able to sense the world with your stick or dog. See, the dog becomes an extension of your sensory apparatus, enabling to help you navigate the world. But if you had your eyes back you would not need this. This pineal gland has been beneficial in the past, when your brains were not so developed, but are not necessary for the way the brain is developing now. Just like everything else, the vibrations enable life to be pieced together and harmoniously intertwined in a way that you could never imagine. ABE.

We would like to say and end today by saying that you are all in control of your own each and individual evolutionary signature. That is being human, and in life sometimes it causes you to be bitter and resentful and closed off from this web of vibrational communication that is now being spun right from the very first thread. It will always be contained within consciousness and therefore the more united it becomes the more this vibrational essence of each and everything harmonises. The more available it is to you, all vibrational alignment, this web of communication will infinitely expand. ABE

27. You have said that some people's brains develop differently, and so block out their natural connections. Has social conditioning within some of our cultures been a deliberate attempt to wire human brains in such a way as to keep people in slumber, so to speak?

This is indeed so. For like we said before, how would they be able to sell your parts back to you if they do not firstly recondition and break it apart in the first place? For you see, it is a game of life in which you have been coaxed into playing and in this you have thought that it is indeed what life is all about. But this is not true, there is so much more to it. It is just that the wiring is all wrong - you see this? You also have to remember your parts in it too, for you have been hypnotized by the highs of modern-day society and when coming back to this it all seems rather dull, rather un-special. But you will see that the one who is awake will indeed see the extraordinary within the ordinary. We know that this is not included within the question, but we would see for it to fit. You see, the DEPRESSION epidemic is one of dissonance because people feel torn between vibrational alignment and the rewiring of the vibrational alignments of the brain. In this you see that now too depression can be a false premise to keep you in this game also, for it will be nurtured and hung around in far too long. Is this of understanding as we know that we may have strayed considerably? ABE.

28. Thank you, ABE. Yes, this is important. If social conditioning is a deliberate attempt to keep people unaware, or in slumber, then is it because there are those in power who understand the truth - the truth of what is ABE and of our connection to Unity-Source? Or is it only because slumbering minds are easier for social management and control?

It is so that people are to use this power in a way to manipulate, and it is also so that people are set - they are not at all interested in getting out of their seats for they have all that they need right here, do they not? Why question it? For you have enough food, even if it is not right for you and the system, but that doesn't matter for you have the little pill to fix it too and in this a great dissonance and a great disservice to all that you are. For some will go an entire lifetime and have never lived a single true moment in their entire life. What a shame. What a waste. ABE.

29. How and why do we experience love?

Ahh, good morning. We see that this is of importance here to convey. Love is a vibration felt by the heart and directed and labelled by the mind or vibration-al signature. You see, all vibrations are felt; they are then filtered through mind or vibrational signature. Your own unique vibrational signature transforms a vibration into a thing; as it is transmuted by it, it is transformed so then that love vibration which was felt say between people was pure consciousness flowing but you labelled it and made it a point of attraction or pinned it upon a certain person or thing. You see, the vibrational signature holds it all; see it like this, you start off with a large lump of clay - we will call it unity or unification or consciousness - you then want to play and make separate things holding it to account with experience. These are the vibrational signatures, what we would like to say is to realise it may seem like different things, but it is still just one thing that being clay. What we would also like to say is that it is not a bad thing to love people and we know in your world that love is very conditioned, where love in reality is unconditioned. It flows, feel it but don't direct it; don't mould the clay and tie it to things and people. ABE.

30. But what about our world of relationships?

We see that this can be confusing. For you would say, if we love all in a way that no-one gets special treat-ment, that you do not have close intimate relation-ships, then you will be destined to be alone. But we do realise that you have a circle in which you are in close proximity. We would never say to not love them in a way that you do. But to know that what you love in them can be extended to a stranger on the other side of the planet and not have to be so contained. It does not have to say that you should love everyone in a way you love your husband or child, but to see that there is no difference in the love that you feel on the transference of it. See, the more you have open-hearted communication and connection with others you realise that you can do nothing but love them. ABE.

31. Why do I not love others and then feel stronger for another?

You see that your vibrational signature can cut this off through past experience. This love is in constant flow, constant motion, when the heart is open but as we say, your vibrational signature wants to open and close and transfers it, filters it through past experience in a way as to protect the organism. You see a person you have all the vibrational conditions and you either allow it or block it. You then match these now feelings to that person or place or thing which in reality was only a memory or a belief and like we say, you let it flow or you allow. ABE.

We would like to add that you see that some people give their love freely to others and some do not. It is all about that vibrational signature. You see, when you first fall in love you are forming this connection. It is allowing universal energy to flow between you unrestricted because you do not yet have any conditions of this love, this connection. As time goes on, you experience more of life together and you bank things in the vibrational signature bank. It gets cluttered and love is not able to flow; it gets stuck within these patterns transferred. What we would like to add is that you can love without possession and love without conditions - you just have to see that. ABE.

32. You discuss love and consciousness as vibrations, and about inter-relationality of all humans. Yet how can we make this knowledge 'real' for people? How can this information help people to live better lives? What can we do?

First and foremost, it is of importance to be human - that is it and that is what we would like to get across. Humans have flaws and accepting them is a way to resonate higher. See, what people think of your so-called enlightened ones is that they have reached a different place, and it is not true at all. The gurus know this; this is why you see so many Buddhist monks smiling, for they see this simplicity of being and how much people struggle because they think that they have to be somewhere higher, that this is not enough. What we say is that it is all here and only the splintered mind cannot see. We would never see to it that you drop your vibrational signature, and we fully understand that this is so ingrained in your experience. What you can really see is that you are not it - you are a long track of vibrations and matter and endless cycles of life and form. In that seeing, in that very knowing, how can one really be splintered? How can one honestly say that they are me and you are you? It cannot be so, and when this is seen as clear as day then, well, you will feel no need to be anywhere other than here, basking in life's undivided beauty. You will do nothing but radiate love and connection for it is all within and therefore will be all around. ABE.

33. Have humans distorted the love energy/vibration in our physical existence? How should it be used? Have human civilizations made use of it differently at other times?

You must see that all vibration is distorted in some way or another in your physical existence - it can be no other way. Like a light that hits an object and bounces off in other directions, it is so with vibration. Now see this, though your own vibrational signature is but built with many differing vibrations, resonating to make one like water that passes through a sieve - whole, separated and whole again, this is so. The pure stream of consciousness flows through the body, through the brain, and is transformed by its conditioned state, by the vibrations that it holds, it is interlinked and also attached too: it is your vibrational signature. We understand that this seems like all individual things, but it is not so. What we are really trying to say is yes, the vibration is always changed by your own vibrational signature. What we are saying is, if you can allow it to flow - and this is done by allowing universal flow - in a way of direct experience of life. See it like this, to have the pure water you would not need a filter; it would not help. The filter may have contaminants that may affect the water which is already pure and in this being more a hindrance. So why not drop the filter, allow pure consciousness to flow by cutting out the unnecessary middleman. This does not mean to be pushed around and passive, but to have direct experience with life. Feel it, be in it, open up your hearts to allow its love. See, in your human form there have and will always be people who try to manipulate this energy flow in a way for self-preservation. But it cannot be done for if it is open heartedly flowing, then you are having direct experience with life. You see the patterns and the self is there but a part of this whole. The only people that know of this and want to manipulate this are the ones who push for self-preservation. ABE.

34. You have stated that ABE is 'zero point.' Does this mean that the ABE collective consciousness is the prime energy that is the source of all things? Is ABE where all physical consciousness manifests from and returns to? Is there anything 'beyond' ABE?

This is so, that we are where all form is and where all form is born from and will eventually fall back too. There is nothing beyond this because there is nothing. For in the nothing you hold everything; it is within the spaces of things that you really have life for. You see this within all your music and language - if there were no space there would be no life. ABE.

35. We all share the same consciousness - we are ABE and ABE is us. We are aspects of ABE in material - or dense vibratory - formation. Is this correct?

That is correct, and we like to keep going back to the Russian doll analogy for it shows that you and only you restrict this flow by means of being engrained and engrossed by the vibrational signature. Hypnotized by all its goings on, treading carefully as not to offend or hurt this vibrational essence; but in the seeing that it is just this it can be let up. ABE.

36. If our consciousnesses are intertwined, then is it possible that you know our questions before we ask them? It is like having a conversation between ourselves?

One could say that yes, for that is how we would see it. Like the whole universe is mad, talking to oneself. But you see, you also do have this vibrational signature for a reason too - for that being there can be a myriad of expressions of just one thing. How wonderful that is to see - we do not say get rid of this but rather allow more in by letting it up. You have become so frightened by it in a way, and in the knowing that it is not really what I am; and 'I am' is a lot more expansive and inclusive. You can realize that life isn't so terrifying, but a great expression of one thing and you can go ahead and just live, just participate. ABE.

37. Is all human thinking a process of receiving/ tapping into this collective consciousness? Is this what is meant by inspiration – what the Greeks called the Muses?

It is so, for when you open up the doll you allow space to flow. It is not another within another but believe us when we say that you are opening up the dolls and are not putting them back together. People are letting up on this vibration but only fear keeps you restricted, for in the fear of loss of self that you will not exist. This has been a vibration from the beginning of time that humans want to say that 'I were here' and that 'I existed' and here is the proof because 'I am me,' but what they do not see is that it is a false identity and if they just let this go a little they will see that there is so much more to be open to, so much more to be receiving. ABE.

38. When artists such as writers or inventors receive their ideas, are they transmitting ideas from the collective consciousness field? If so, is it not the case that ideas have been seeded through such channels to help to evolve human civilization?

These are great questions and we feel that there need not to be such drawn out answers from us for we see that you are of great understanding for you are very allowing of this flow. For in your own work you have but help open minds and create foundations for evolutionary steps forward. We have a question to you - how does one feel when writing of these things? Do you feel yourself, or that you are allowing something other? ABE.

39. As an example, popular science-fiction books and films are sometimes used to manifest and distribute ideas for later possible actualization?

This is true, for sometimes it is great to get a message across by a song or a film or a book for this widens the scope to which people are touched by these things. See it like this, as in the previous question, the whole universe talking to itself to be able to know itself. These things set in motion as little pointers to wake you up like alarm clocks dotted all about the universe. ABE.

40. How does this relate to Carl Jung's theory of the collective unconscious?

Very well, for was he not just doing the same and bringing this universal consciousness into being through his own vibrational signature and in this he let up on his own vibrational signature to allow that of the one consciousness to flow? ABE.

41. You have previously stated that 'there are others who are resonating highly but maybe are not of the world.' Could you clarify what you mean by this?

We would mean so in the term of not your world, and of the planets you are yet to discover. See, all is at differing evolutionary stages, and this is of harmony. ABE.

42. Does ABE distinguish itself from other communications that have been 'channelled'?

To us we would feel like this is and has been of use to those whom seek that way. But for us it is really of being human - we do not want to take you to our being for what would be the point? But it is more so of a seeing and realization of how great and wonderful it really is to be in form. There have been so many that have tried to take you away from this by trying to reach a higher state. What we feel is that it now needs to be grounded and brought right back down to Earth for it really to be of any use to humanity. ABE.

43. Many traditions talk about 'higher consciousness' – what they really mean is a rise in the resonance of one's vibrational signature? Is this rise coming to everyone as part of natural evolution? Is there a method whereby a person could individually accelerate this vibrational shift?

Good morning, we are happy to have this continued connection with you both. Higher consciousness is indeed that way, not a higher place to get to but a resonance in which you are more accustomed to be - more open to receive. Now see here, we do not mean for a person to have to resonate at a certain point like you really have to do anything. It is of the notion of coming to grips with that in which you are. There is never anywhere to get to, just a knowing of that this is how it is. Now if you are asking as to move this along more quickly, then it is really just in the allowance of this knowledge; really getting to realize and understand that this is how it is so - by truly experiencing it and done by allowing it to flow. ABE.

44. What is the role of DNA within human evolution? Is it also a vibrational code? What is the function of the majority of unknown DNA once referred to as 'junk DNA?'

Ah yes, it does indeed make us laugh at the word junk for is it not in the knowing that something to be of use and is now not? Well, this is not so; it is just that your sciences indeed are not able at this point of your evolution to decode that at which they are not open to. You see, the more open you are to this flow, these vibrations, the more you let go of your very constricting conscious mind. You know that when you let up a little space you allow something to move and in this you are able to not only understand but clearly see. Your DNA is very much the vibrational code of life - it is vibrational memory. Like we discussed earlier, one big conversation going on but to itself. One could see it like this: you have your parent's vibrational signature and through this you create and wind these two seemingly different vibrations and create a new vibration. This is but the structure of your DNA. ABE.

45. In our physical reality right now there are a lot of problems with obesity and food-related illnesses. There are also an unprecedented amount of chemicals in our food production. Are we creating greater dissonance with our bodies?

But of course, this is so for you are trying to control and conquer something you do not have the whole picture of. For if you really could understand yourselves then you would indeed not want to put the things you do so into your bodies. The harmony of the body cannot leave out that of your environment in its natural state. For you are mixing up the vibrational alignment by trying to straighten it all. But you see, you do not need to do so for in the straightening out of a wiggly line you are flatlined. You kill it - do you see that this so makes sense?

46. What can you say about the rise of genetically modified food sources? Some people consider them our future - should they be introduced into our food systems?

We see that there are many people on your planet and believe that as this continues to grow there will be more of a need for growth in your food production. What you do not see is that by making these modifications to your food you are indeed making these modifications to your planet and in turn the cosmos - it is always inter-relational. There will always be ways in which life will cause you as a human species to modify life, to upgrade to solve, and this is indeed good. But in the seemingly extreme concentration on one area you automatically denounce another. It needs to be more open and understanding of these vibrational essences of life and the inter-relational connection of everything. For if this is understood clearly you can do nothing but automatically move forward and in this flourish. ABE.

47. How important is physical exercise? Should we know our bodies better? Practices such as yoga are popular now – are these good ways to develop body alignment and resonance?

Mm, yes; see exercise as so an interaction of seemingly two separate things. You see, your ancestors moved all day long until it was time to not do so; and we know that advancement in technology has caused many to be very stagnant and still. A lot of times throughout the day in this you are not allowing this energy to flow; you are not connected, for when you are stagnant it is so that energy is stagnant. This actually slows down and lowers your vibrational signature. See this, though no movement is better than any other it is purely just movement needed if your vibrational signature is matched to that. To do yoga - by all means do that. You will indeed get much from it, but if it is not so then it will be of no use VIBRATIONALLY. See, we discussed this resonance earlier with you talking about food and then your being is begrudging of not having a different food. As such, it may well be good for the mechanics of the body, but the vibrational alignment will be out of whack. Health will never be healthy until you take on board that you are also very much a vibrational being. You can take care of the mechanics, but you also need to take care of your vibrational signature. This meaning, you also take on the vibrational signature of that in which you eat. We are not denouncing these great ways of getting people moving as they do indeed also make people aware of their own energy etc. What we are saying, that no one is better than any other form of movement providing you are aware that you are also vibrational. ABE.

48. Greater numbers of people are suffering from addictions, especially alcohol and drug related. How are these issues related with the times we are living in?

They are in a way to escape this - that you have been so tightly focused on self and how and what you should be doing and being that you look out on a world that is tough and disconnected and lonely. You see, all these things do, really, are allowing you to drop you in a way. You are not that, and many people know this, but society is saying you have to uphold this idea of you, or you will not survive. You will not succeed, and the dissonance is caused and when dissonance is caused you want to escape this. It is so very sad but so true, and we are not saying that you should feel sorry for people who use drugs or alcohol, for there are many who do not so but are maybe obsessed with changing lovers or addicted to food or sex or working. See, anything can be an addiction in a sense, to escape this life. I suppose it is just what people are going to choose as their vice. ABE.

49. Diseases such as cancer have increased dramatically in recent years. Why is this?

We can say but two words and that is - vibrational dissonance. We feel so very strongly to convey this at this time as we see it ravaging the body of many, taking countless lives. It always starts off as dissonance, always. ABE.

50. There is a lack of understanding about death in our modern societies. It feels as if we need to see it as a transition stage rather than as the end. What are your comments on this?

See, death will always be so that it is hard to grasp, and of mourning for many who do not understand the part of that in which you are. Clearly, you have some emotional attachment to say of a dear friend or of a loved one. It will always be so, and you would need to let that vibrational part of you come up and express for there is never any sense in pushing it down. You do not need to become unattached to life. You see, in the beauty of that heartfelt release of another, you feel alive. That is beauty, that is part of being human. What we would like to say that this is not the end. It is of the body as it cannot continue, but your vibrational signature is always in the mix, always. It is like making a cake: many ingredients make up on thing a cake. That is what we can say as to life after death. You see, people saying that they have a near-death experience and they may well see a light, for the signature is still there; it is still running through, but it is still very much a human thing. When you have no body you are no longer splintered - you are back to wholeness, that is it. ABE.

51. Continuing the theme of understanding the end-of-life transition. Could you say something about the process that occurs after the death of the physical body?

The end of your body is not the end of life, just a change in form, for you always go back to the whole. What we really want you to see in your human form is that you are a cycle; that you are this wholeness. There is deep beauty in this process. There has been much fear around death, and it is understandable in a way as your mind works in the polarities of life. You see, this vibrational essence of who you are is a part of this wholeness. It is not soul - you do not leave the body. The body changes form. The vibrational signature that was once blank in a sense, or zero, is now going back to the pool of pure consciousness. Life is a process and there are always different stages. The vibrational signature does not leave, it just hasn't the bodily reso-nation to sustain it, for it to be stagnant, so it returns back to the source. But hear this, it does not become lost. It is a collection, but not of physicality, like a soul - a wholeness in life or consciousness constantly expressing itself, constantly talking to itself. Does this explain it well?

52. What can you say about the concept of reincar-nation? Do particular vibrational signatures return to form to continue with life experiences?

One could say that you have all lived every life for it would be silly to say that wholeness or oneness has not lived all lives - so this is of truth. What we would like to say is that there are also resonation of the vibrational signature. You see, your religion is very much based upon a physical entity of sorts that would lord upon man to be good and moral, so religion imposed the idea of a cycle coming back and back until you finally get it right. There is some truth in a sense that life is cyclic, but no truth in that it is to get this life right. You see, that is very much a human concept; for if you are not thriving in this life surely you could then be in the other world. But there is no other world, and to some this can be disheartening. There is just one world in different expressions and that one world is the whole thing - the whole show, for it cannot be any other way. So, we wanted to express to you that if there was a matching of vibration, one would see this as the soul cycling around and around. But it is not the continuance of a person to another, for an essence of your passed ones is in the world, in everything. There are specific signatures that attract signatures of another type, but it is not of you going into another body neatly packaged to live again. It is not this way at all but essence. Some might think that with this information humans would be lost but it is not so, for you will fully see that all is of you and that there is no definition. ABE.

53. Why does vibrational consciousness come or 'birth' into form? Are we here to have specific lessons or experiences?

Life moves, life cycles, life is change and life is consciousness. We would like to say that although religion and society has taught you in a way that you are here for lessons or experiences, it is not this way. You see, the thing that you call soul does not have to reach a higher state for it to be accepted with open arms and to say 'good job.' No, the overall point of all of this, the whole point of us being here, is to wake you up to that of which you already are. You are an expression of one complete thing, so to say. That you are here for lessons would in some way say that you are not already what you are. Here is a little story: a baby kangaroo abandoned by his mother was taken in by a pack of hyenas. Now all was good and well until one day the grown kangaroo bumped into another kangaroo. The other kangaroo hopped off and the kangaroo was in awe of this creature. He went about trying to be like the kangaroo but could not be, until one day the hyenas came clean and he was told that he too was a kangaroo like the one he had seen and in that moment of knowing he was able to hop and jump just like the others. You see, it isn't about lessons - it is more so about remembrance, like connecting back up the phone line that you had left off the hook. Again, so you are connected to all that you are. You see, you always have everything you need - you just need to see that. ABE.

54. Could you explain if there is a difference between what we call pure consciousness, soul, and spirit?

No, all but the one same thing - and we would be even reluctant to call it anything other than this zero-state. But do hear this, soul and spirit are that too of vibrational signature. But you see, that they are but one thing - albeit the row of identical flowers that each have their own scent. Is this of understanding?

55. You have said that disease is a result of vibrational dissonance. Could you explain more on this?

Vibrational dissonance is when two vibrations are rejecting or repelling each other. They are not harmonizing; they are not attracting each other BUT also there are more dominant vibrations. Say, a heavier vibration, a denser vibration compared to something that is just okay. See this, when you walk into a room and there has been an argument you feel the density in that room. You feel as though your whole being is weighted upon - this is the true meaning of dark energy. So, in regards to disease, dissonance is caused by two seemingly different vibrations trying to be held at the same time. Take it like this, you hate broccoli. You had a bad experience and was extremely sick when you were a child eating some. Now the doctor comes along and says that broccoli is the only thing that will make you better today. You have complete vibrational dissonance. See, life as you experience it and in this your own vibrational signature is being wound together. The body always wants to work in harmony, always, but it does that by vibration; by talking to each part vibrationally. This vibration is and always needs to be in resonance to that of which you are, and also that of your environment. But you see, it is not so. For example, you could eat something that is factory made, that is dead. In a way it is vibrationally talking to the cells, to communicate that in which your environment is like. In this, the vibrational signature will be lowered because it tells the cells to act in a certain way. But see this, if you are eating only organic food and your own internal vibration is not a match to this, this also creates dissonance. There was a lady whom only ate fresh organic fruits and vegetables, never smoked or drank, exercised regularly, and still died at the age of 35 from a heart attack. This was because her vibrational dissonance was caused by the vibrational signature she had due to her heartache. She was so focused on her health and wellbeing she forgotten about her relationships, and in this she felt that dissonance in her heart. Life is always about balance - always. ABE.

56. You state that DNA is the vibrational code of life. Could you explain more about the role of DNA? Also, how does DNA relate with consciousness? Will human science come to work more with the properties of human DNA - and how?

DNA is the building blocks of life, it is true. For in this vibrational code you have all the knowledge of who you are. You see many new age groups saying that you can wake up your DNA for the codes for activation of higher consciousness, and this is true. But see this, it only carries what is up to now, and presuming that you are not fully evolved then you can see that there is point at which you will get right back to here. But see this, DNA is also a receiver of vibrational code, so you are creating new vibrational code by your own being. You contain vibrational code from that of which you have come and evolved from, but also you can receive new DNA structure by opening up to this one consciousness. As you see, this is evolution; this is the way in which your species allows itself to take the steps forward. Is this of understanding?

57. You have said that humans can receive new DNA structure as part of their evolution. Is this similar to, say, receiving a new program 'update' that provides new information for developing? Could you say more on this?

It is in the creation of these pathways so it is but put into the program to pass on a memory bank of evolution. Is this of understanding? For when new DNA is then created it is binding together what is two resonances and creating but one new; and one could say and hopefully would be improved, evolved. Hear this though, it is also a receiver of what is. ABE.

58. You stated that 'many new age groups saying that you can wake up your DNA for the codes for activation of higher consciousness' and this is true - up to a point. Could you clarify more on this? Thank you.

It is true in a way that you can awaken that in which has been and what is already present. It is not true to awaken pure consciousness. You do not need to activate it but allow this vibration. In this you see, it is molding together past, present, and future ancestry vibration - your vibration and that of pure consciousness. Is this of understanding?

59. In that case, is it really necessary to have New Age groups performing these rituals like a service? Can we not allow this activation/flow ourselves through our own intention? Is there a personal method for this?

This is what we want you to see. It is a very human condition to put power outside of yourself. There really is no need for this - it is indeed through your own knowing. You really do have to start to pick up the pieces that have always set you apart and really start putting this cosmic puzzle back together to wholeness. We are in no way denouncing these practices for they do awaken people to be more open, but many get so caught up in it. ABE.

60. Is DNA the code of life for the cosmos? If so, how does DNA function for other planets and other species?

You see also that DNA resonates and picks up your vibrational code. It's like a get together of past, present, and future, and then deciding what to build its foundations on. It is the code of life on all planets and works exactly the same for all species all over the cosmos. ABE.

61. How did DNA originate? Was it 'developed' in some way?

DNA is but the code of life, the building blocks in physical form to pass on that at what stage you are but at. As you are moving into less of a physical evolution and more so of a conscious one, you will see that DNA is also a receiver of vibration enabling it to be built and to bring together that which resonates, an attraction of such. For from the very first building block was born but from the one thing but enabled it to become split and in this it was breaking down into smaller and smaller parts, marrying parts together through resonation. For the first whisper of life it was born into be that something of separation. But you see, it was not just an expression, a dance of life. Is this of understanding?

62. In terms of bodily health, is it expected that human life spans are going to increase as part of our future evolution?

This will be so, for your life span is always increasing due to the technological advances and the more complex the brain becomes. You see, these vibrations create new neural pathways, new connections, and in this building a new structure. This means you will become more complex. Your bodies will not be so dense as the vibrational essence rises on your planet, and in this will allow the system to thrive for longer. But see this, technology will be a large part of your futures. You will have morphed in a way to be part machine and this will work, say, when you lose a limb or something dramatic happens to the body - it is of use then. What we would like to say is that in this vibrational evolution, this one of consciousness, it will be evident that you will live longer, for the body will not be so pressured - the vibrational signature will not be so dense. ABE.

63. Human sexuality in terms of gender roles seems to be shifting, and blurring. Many people are finding that to be either 'male' or 'female' does not fit into their physical and psychological well-being. Is this related to our current evolutionary shifts? Could you comment on this?

Ahh, we see this and would like to say but one thing - social conditioning. For in the splitting of say more and more genders you are but casting the net of more separation. The people who do not classify that they are but one or the other are so just saying 'I am human, and love is love and this is it.' We see that things get lost - why not be that of being human? ABE.

SECTION THREE – Human Society & Culture

1.What is your knowledge and perspective upon our history here on this planet?

But of course, every vibrational signature, every experience, has come back to this. But hear this, you know all that is - you are able to always tap into this knowledge by allowing it to flow by unification. We are not something outside of you. Take, for example, the Wizard of Oz, the great old wise wizard of Emerald City, knower of all. But honestly, when you pull back the veil, just a normal man. You only limit yourselves by shutting out that in which you are. For if it is not of substance then it does not exist. Tell us, what does it mean to you to exist?

If you are but asking us to reel off history, then we can say this - there has been great famine, destruction, cities found and lost, civilizations come and go, and this will be so again. Your planet and the cosmos are in constant flux, and the ones who resist and hold so tightly to what they believe, and cannot move forward with this, will surely not be able to keep their own heads above water due to the new vibrations, due to this new energy. We say new in a sense of that it is new to your form right now. This is what has happened before, and it will surely continue. ABE.

2. Thank you. You say we need to keep our head above water due to the new vibrations. What can you tell us about these 'new vibrations?' Are we going to experience a period of increased disruption?

We say new in a sense that it is new to your physical bodies of this time and space. We would like to say that these vibrations and energies are manifesting at great intensity and there will be ones that fight hand and tooth to keep things the way they are now. You see, when the seed is cracked open it could be seen as completely destructive, when in essence it is bringing new life. For the new life to come forth, the old shell that contained this new life will have to crack open and this will be extremely destructive. For the more this energy is brought forth, or we prefer 'allowed,' you are tapping it in and grounding it down into this reality. In this, it will shake away all that has been built, and in this you will see that the ones who cannot walk this path will not be able to succeed. ABE.

To answer if there is increased disruption, we would say yes; as there are many that are grounding this vibration. They are unifying this of us and that of you, so the more people do this the more it will be destructive for the systems in place now. When you see more disruption, you will know that more people are enabling unification. ABE.

3. Are there ways in which people could better 'ground' this vibration and new energy? How can people consciously assist in allowing this energy vibration in?

The unification: by knowing what you are, not allowing too much baggage, too many human conditions. Our very work is to show you that you are it; that there is not a stagnant self that lords upon the world but a process of life - a united field of existence. If we can get this across to as many as possible; if they feel it in their very essence and truly deeply embody this truth, then wow - change will manifest in even the darkest of corners and it will light up all that is still hiding in the shadows. ABE.

4. We would like to assist your work too. Please indicate to us how we can best do this. Is it good for us to continue with our questions - does this assist the process?

It does assist very well, as we feel these are very appropriate to the things that people will ask and want to know; and we feel that sometimes we denounce or dismiss. But this is from a place of pure love and not to be of 'I know' and 'you do not' for we state that all this is what you are. It is really to loosen the grips you have and although you are very much loose in your grip, your mind gets lost in the language - in the naming and pinpointing of particular things. What we would like you to truly feel is this. Tell us, what allows for your inspiration to flow, for you to feel connected?

5. Some traditions have a cyclic understanding of development, such as the Vedic Yuga cycles. They say we pass from an Iron Age to a Golden Age. Could you comment on this understanding?

There will always be cycles, and we believe there are many names for this. With the one you state in your question we understand to be of an already established structure. We are not to denounce your structures and your beliefs but to loosen the grip. See, you get so very lost in language; naming this, making it stagnant, pinpointing, separating. Our basis is always unification. If this can fit into the idea that you have for unification, then it is of use. If not, dismiss it. ABE.

6. Some theories state that planetary evolution occurs according to electromagnetic cycles, or other cosmic energy cycles. What can you say about this?

We will always state that this is true - but to what notion do you have of cycles? It is built upon structures of old that have so much baggage tied to them.

For life is really cyclic; you know this, you are forever becoming but never getting to see things. Never stop and start, just change, interact, morph, but never a specific time or place. Science does like to pinpoint a cause and effect. But you see, when you pinpoint one interaction you forget about the others that have led it to this, and then to the ones before. Does this answer this?

7. What would be a more correct way to consider evolution upon this planet? How are humanity a part of this evolutionary process?

We would say that evolution is always vibratory. We go back to the Russian doll analogy. For you to have your own planetary evolution, it has a knock-on effect to other places in the cosmos. And for their evolution it is also the same for you; it is so tightly inter-woven that to pinpoint this evolutionary process you would have to go right back to unification. And to see the end result, you would see also unification; and in this you can see the pattern of the forever becoming. Can you not?

8. Can humans delay or interfere with the planet's evolution, or is it out of our hands? Current thinking says that we are disturbing evolution (climate change) or advancing it (geo-engineering). Yet isn't this hubris?

There is a very fine line to tread here. We would like to say yes, you can interfere, but not so much in a way of physical action. It needs to be of this conscious, this vibratory action. You see, there will be many who will denounce this knowledge just so that they can be active in the world - active being in the physical sense. And although we see a time to be in action, we also see the need to be from no action; for you to then take the correction from a place of truth - your truth. ABE.

9. It has been said that for the past ten thousand years we have had the possibility for conscious evolution - that is, our species evolution can move ahead through deliberate, conscious, directed effort. Can you comment on this?

You see, to have something conscious, now you really have to allow. Being conscious is the key to this unification. It is an allowing of pure consciousness to be present in this time-space reality. It is who you are. We don't expect you to slay your vibrational signature or dismiss it at all, for this is also the creative essence of consciousness. It is about bringing together the two. You see, your unconsciousness is your vibrational signature and when you are not conscious it runs the show. But by being conscious, you allow these two to unify; not ridding of any one, just allowing what you are and what you think you are to exist in this time-space. But see this, they are never not flowing; but you can be unaware and lost in the unconscious, never knowing that there is so much more to your being. Does this answer the above?'

10. So, what you are saying is that by allowing pure consciousness to flow through us and into our reality - onto the planet - we are assisting with the evolutionary process. We don't need to struggle to assist evolution. On the contrary, we should learn to allow it all to flow and to ground it? To use an analogy, the human species is like a vibratory, resonating membrane - or skin - for the planet?

You need to stop resisting evolution. Stating this is not how it is meant to look. You see, this theme is in much of your life. By allowing, you sync up with the knowing that your way is not necessarily the right way. ABE.

11. So, what you are saying is that by allowing pure consciousness to flow through us and onto the planet we are assisting with the evolutionary process?

That is but so. You are, but not distorting it so much but see this - like light hitting any physical thing it will bounce off in all directions expressing in different ways. This is so, but true of this too. ABE.

12. As all planetary evolution is interwoven, would it not be disastrous for the cosmos if humans destroyed or greatly damaged the Earth, such as through nuclear war?

Oh, but of course. For unification does not hold place for war. For in the unification knowledge, you understand that what you do is only but done upon you. ABE.

13. The phenomenon of crop circles has intrigued many people. There is the hypothesis that these are messages being given to us to help our understanding. Could you comment on this phenomenon?

Ahh, the crop circles. Now see this, there have always been signals, interventions, for we live in a unified field of consciousness. There will always be pointers, and symbolism has been used throughout the whole cosmos. And although you may not understand it, it can be decoded. We would be more inclined to think that it has come from a human tapping into or being of this energy source, rather than a little green man flying in. You see, it takes a lot for other species to enter your dense atmosphere; and even more so, for they do not want to be seen to interfere physically as to impose or direct. Is this of understanding?

14. Many areas of the planet are known as sacred sites or 'energy' sites - such as Stonehenge in the UK. Did our ancestors have specific knowledge of cosmic energy? Could you say more about Earth's energy sites or energy lines?

There are such sites. But hear this, they are no more sacred than your back yard. You can tap into this anywhere. There was in your earlier conscious evolution specific points, and only because they built up the intention to connect in a certain spot did it become a portal or a place to connect. You see, if what we are saying is true - that all is unified - then how can it not be here and there and wherever you go?

15. You say that such sacred sites are no more sacred than our back yard. This is good to know. Yet what about certain energetic 'hot spots' – such as sacred buildings (Alhambra, meditation halls or tekkias) – that are said to connect and facilitate energy flow. Are these places not more conducive to the flow of pure consciousness?

No, they are not at all. They may have this sense that they are, so people are to believe that it is so and therefore build up intention of it being so. It can be felt because of the people and the resonance of connection, not because of the place. ABE.

16. What can you say about energy lines that crisscross the planet? Some of these are well-known and may be pilgrim routes. Others are said to connect specific places. Are these not like planetary neural connections?

Like we said, it could be so likened to that, yes. They are of but conscious communication talking of and to itself - vibrational resonance, a membrane as such. Is this of understanding?

17. Have other intelligences, or species, been involved with assisting the evolution of this planet? If so, in what ways? Has there been knowing human collaboration with other intelligences? Why is this subject so taboo in our societies?

It is so taboo for you do not understand yourselves. It would be spoken of if you could so get to a place whereas you knew all that you are. For in the knowing of oneself, you are knowing that of which you are. If you know this, then you can see that it is all a part of you, and it would not have so much fear. For humans think that they have to impose their way only because they are not consciously aware. But do you honestly think that other species that are more evolved think in this way? It is not so. If you are asking if other species have assisted, it has only been when people have opened up to this, an intention if you will. ABE.

**18. Developed societies have entered an acceler-
ated phase of materialism and consumption. This
is stimulated by corporate greed. Is this a sign
of our old systems and will this pass? Did other
civilizations also pass through a phase of intense
materialism?**

Your existence, like we say, is one of cyclic motion. It
is but an outdated system of consumerism; but understand, it will never be completely rid of it for even in
the waking up to this there will always be a form of
consumption in human nature. You are right to say
that it has been completely monopolized by some that
are based in greed. But this too is balancing itself. Your
job is to be awake and conscious of it. Now there have
always been civilizations that have taken too much,
and in this, resources dwindle. What happens is that
the Earth will bring it back to balance. Really, all you
need to be is aware - the planet knows its own balance
like you do with your own body, if you are aware. We
would like to add that yes, humans find a resource and
they take it and they see that it is beneficial and in this
it is monetized. And although this is not true for how
other civilizations conducted their affairs, it is still in
some sense of truth. But you see, it does balance itself
back out when people awaken and connect. ABE.

**19. The population on the planet has accelerat-
ed dramatically within the last century. We will
reach 9 or 10 billion people by 2050. There are
some fears of over-population. Is this accelerat-**

ed population part of our current development? Some people are worried about this. What is your perspective?

Over-population is always of keen interest. Look at it like this, if the soil is fertile you would have a good crop. You need space between these crops, so they are able to truly flourish, to be able to maximize the growth of the plant. You see, when over-population occurs the space is clearly getting smaller; your cities are built higher and your countryside is expanded, and land is taken to accommodate more people. We always come back to it, but balance is key, and people to resources is of essence. When you upset this balance by, like you say, over-population you are putting these crops closer together. You are manufacturing foods that are not built for consumption. Everything becomes quick and more, and in this a great dissonance is served. It really is a knock-on effect, a cycle, and you are it. We would also like to state that as life spans of humans expands this will also cause problems in regards to your population. You see, with this kind of problem there is no obvious solution other than restrictions in place formed by society. But we would like to say but one thing - this new energy that is upon your civilization has to resonate to that of the system. If not, you will not be able to go forward in this physical existence. This is all we would like to say on this for now. ABE.

20. Our political systems are largely corrupt, and people are losing their trust and respect in them. We are due for a dramatic change. Is this part of the necessary transformation required upon this planet at this time?

It is. As more and more people awaken, they will see that indeed things are not in balance, are off. Like you have been so conditioned in a way. As more and more people come back round, in a sense they will see. But see this, people will be outraged and disappointed and angry like they have been betrayed and hypnotized and befooled, and you will see all this mayhem and pushing back. You know, we like to say that you can never fight the old by fighting it. You are keeping it there in prominent position. What does the person who wants to force their way always want? It is a reaction, a resistance, an argument but that will not solve the matter. We really want you to claim all yourselves back before you can take a step forwards - to action this is our purpose and it is also yours. ABE.

21. The global finance system seems to be a manipulated and 'rigged' system that favours the specialist financial players. Yet the flow of money is also an important system of energetic exchange. What can you say about this?

It is an important energetic exchange and has always been so, albeit in many different forms over time. We would say that this exchange is coming to an end of physical money as you know it. You will be going forward with a digital currency in which you can see firmly taking place and rooting as we speak. There will be people who claim more and channel it in a way so that it benefits a few manipulating and directing this system. But you see, as more people get wise to this, the more they can claim it back. You see, many coming together is a lot more powerful than the one holding the bunch of notes alone. They will not have power or place to manipulate if people unite. That is why they push to keep things splintered, people disconnected. A united nation is a powerful force. ABE.

22. There is a lot of talk now about digital currency - it can be used for greater transparency as well as greater control. Will digital currency not just replace the old system and maintain the same inequalities and struggles?

Not if people are awake for it can be directed in a sense as to barter, to exchange goods for goods, not to accumulate and take stock of. It just will not be in the sense as what currency is now. It cannot continue this way. ABE.

Our whole stripping back to basics is for us an un-conditioning of what you have for so long seen yourselves to be. Because other humans have placed them upon you, it is time to in a sense break free from the hysteria and come back to oneself - if you are ever able to unite. ABE.

23. There are many people who view that the world is really governed by a small group of elites who are holding on to their power. Can people really make a change through their individual efforts or consciousness?

Like we say, it is not something that can be fought. You see this with many things now. But hear this - people are waking up but are also falling into another trap of consumerism and political disconnection, thinking that always they have to pick a side when there is no side to pick and all is worn out. Then you may see, but we are coming forth to hopefully make you see a lot sooner. For if left too late, everything else will have been completely exhausted. ABE.

24. At this current time our societies are becoming more authoritarian and controlling – especially through technology. Are we moving more toward control societies? Will this not cause conflict with the free flow and expression of consciousness?

Someone who is not awake will always want to control, for if a person is truly awake, and we mean truly, they will feel no need for domination whatsoever. Now, to say if you are moving forward to a more controlled society the answer could be yes. But you see, in this suppression, this pressing something down, it will at some point have no other choice but to bounce back. ABE.

25. Propaganda and forms of social conditioning seem to be very high and there are great efforts directed into this. At the same time, you speak about individual power within each of us. How do you view this situation?

You see, it is like this; a tug-of-war pushing and pulling, always trying to get the little knotted red line to the centre of the line. You see, we are not saying that life should be euphoric, and it should be likened to that of heaven. If there is a heaven then it is here with you now, and the same with hell. You see, you are human and there are interactions and individual vibrational signatures and much more. What we want you to see as clear as day is that in which you truly are. Truly take it all back, all those feelers that state you are this and you need that and on and on - such a tiresome existence. It is in the realization that 'oh I am here, and I am also that but I can be this' - and share it. Isn't that an existence? Isn't that the true beauty of a human life? Society does indeed dumb you down and cut you into so many pieces for if it didn't so, then how would they be able to sell you your fragments back? ABE.

26. You have stated that we need to realize that we are everything – we are 'it.' Yet is this really enough to create change within our societies? To know something does not always result in tangible internal transformation.

The transformation will only come when you realize this. For if you do not break such a constricted pattern of being, then how will you ever see any change? We are never saying to not act but acting from the same patterns are never going to create different results. There will never be change and you see this in many of your worldly affairs. ABE.

27. The majority of people upon this planet have not yet 'awakened' to the truth. They prefer to watch television, or play their games. Do you see this situation changing? Will the newer energies arriving on this planet create some dissonance here?

Yes, it will, for it is like there is something in the air - like a nice smell of say fresh baked bread and they see that 'oh I am in life again.' They start to feel and shake off the monotony of just being and start living. But see this, it is much easier to sit back down and numb-out again because people are so afraid to feel, to love, and to live. What a shame! If only they knew that – wow – this is what I can do. I feel hurt but in this I am alive, I am here, I am participating. Such beauty in this realization. ABE.

28. Our technologies now connect us across the globe. We are communicating like never before. Would you say the Internet is a reflection of our own internal connectivity? How do you envision the development of the Internet?

It is a physical adaptation of that in which you are. It is showing you in physical form to unite, to communicate, to interact. The same as when the phone was invented - it had the same effect, bringing this energy that no-one could conceive at all and putting it into your physical existence for you to believe it and use it. Now, for people who are able to adapt to this new energy or allowance there will not be such a need for these physical technologies. It is some time off, but you as humans will be connecting and allowing this flow of communication. See this, the heart is the connector vibrationally and the head is the receiver - just like a phone line. If these are both open to receive then it will be that way. ABE.

29. It seems that upon this planet humanity is evolving toward a planetary civilization. Is this so? Does this suggest we are moving toward a world government? Is this shift to greater centralization a part of the civilizing pattern, and has this occurred on other planets?

We would like to see this movement towards a united government, yes. But see this, we have said before that even you, as your own vibrational essence, does not need to be rid of it, is truly, truly in the undoubtable knowing of unification. If this is so, then we would hope that there would be no need to be governments but just humans. It has happened on other planets; but you see, they are a different species and different formations and have resonated different from the start so have not conducted things the same. They too have made mistakes and are in no way superior, just more evolved. ABE.

30. Human societies place many layers of social conditioning upon their citizens. People adopt belief systems, ideologies, etc. Are you saying it is necessary to de-condition ourselves, and if so how might we go about this?

Good morning both - we are pleased to see this continued connection. Your human society is but built upon social conditioning. It really does take you further down the rabbit hole. Its outdated structure is just that – outdated. It does not and will not resonate with the new wave, the new vibration. This is why things can look destructive for in the holding onto old outdated structures, one tends to get aggravated and at dissonance. You see, this new vibration people are feeling like we said 'the winds of change' but they are not sure what it is. This is where we would like to come in and lend a helping hand or more, so both in physical form, this connection - these words - will resonate with many, for we wanted to get it down to the bare bones again, no nonsense. The way to de-condition is by needs of allowing this flow of energy. Allowing the heart to open and allowing the mind to be free. This will take work, for hearts have become closed and also that of minds, which you know is your vibrational signature. Loosen the grip on the story of 'me' and try to allow the story of 'we' - of unity. ABE.

31. Human civilization on this planet is currently at the phase of nation states and nation-blocks. Yet isn't this a limited stage that we need to supersede and isn't nationalism a limiting vibration-pattern? Could you comment on this?

But of course. It is as we said above, people feel this need to hang onto something, to grab a hold of their identity. Some tie it to their country, some to their football team. See, people live a lot in fear - in fear that people will take what they have, their status, their belongings, their identity. When they feel threatened in this way they fight back and want to claim what is rightfully theirs. See it like this, your media puts a spanner in the works; by the end of this the whole factory is shut down wanting to never see a spanner in their factory ever again! What they do not realize is that the spanner contributes, and it was put there in such a way as to cause aggravation and separation. Is this of understanding of what we try to put to you?

32. There is a growing trend toward increased urban living – larger cities and more mega-cities. We feel that there should be a balance and more

rural living. Is it not important to cultivate agrarian lifestyles and to live off the land?

See this, in an ideal world people would be more self-sufficient, cultivating the land and going off-grid. But you see, many people are not wanting to take this route. They like their cities and cafe's and hustle and bustle. What you can create though in these places are more natural spots, more open spaces: roof top farming, a box on the window, community projects, connection to each other and the world around. For this would be of great benefit and you see people coming together again already doing such things. In the Second World War supplies were limited, people were taught to work their land again, cultivating what they have, growing what they could. This was forced upon people and although we do not like the idea of directing, we do feel that there will be a time in which this will be implemented again due to population spikes. ABE.

33. Should more people consider living 'off-grid' – that is, more independent and sustainable lifestyles? Is this a good future direction despite it going contrary to current trends?

It would be, yes. But we would like to see it more community focused for it not only gives connection to your world but to each other - working together, cultivating together, sharing the food. For the best meal of the day is really the one shared with those you love, is it not? ABE.

34. Despite our high levels of connectivity, more people are becoming strangers to their neigh-bours. Does not the sense of unification also apply to our human communities? Will current trends not also trigger a rise in alternative communities?

Yes, this is the way we see it going - for in unification you cannot but move into a more community focused setting. People would say that they would not feel good to be in a commune, but it will not exactly be like that. More so, a gathering of communities working togeth-er. You will see this far more so when your currency that you have now is no longer of use. You see, people think that in this sense of doing this you will be taking a step backwards. But it is not so. There will be deeper connection in this to your world, to each other, and also to that of your instinctual human nature. You cannot shut out that in which you are - and believe us when we say you have been running away from this truth for some time now, through fear of stagnation and no progression. But this also is a falsity. ABE.

35. Heart communication is a strong vibration and creates harmonic resonance. What social or cultural activities would help to promote this harmonic resonance?

Connection – open-hearted connection - this is only implemented when you drop the vibrational signa-ture, the conditioning. See it like a heavy bag that disallows you to open your arms and embrace life. For when you put it down, not get rid but stop trying to uphold it, you feel your arms free to embrace life and each other. This is the way of the open heart and this is when true connections are made. ABE.

36. Are sporting activities a form of developing teamwork and harmonic resonance? Has sport been used on this planet as a channel, or vehicle, for promoting higher vibrations amongst our species?

It is in a way, yes. Team work is important, but you see it is still quite limiting in a sense that even though society has built teams it still separates by way of stating my team is better than your team, and in that sense you are not better off at all. The idea is one of a global team, and although it sounds euphoric it is not. The one cause that all can be working towards and what you all share is humanity. ABE.

37. Our cultures promote values of competition, conquest, and control. We sense that we need our vibrational influence to shift to values of collaboration, communication, and compassion. Will these values be more dominant in our younger and upcoming generations?

Yes, but of course. They are born into this vibration. It is so different for these - they will be the way-bearers if allowed to do so, guided and not suppressed by their peers. You see the younger taking a stance, not fearful of dominant structures. This is good - this is change. ABE.

38. There have been major migrations of people across the planet in recent years. This cultural mix of diversity has many advantages, and yet it instills fear in many people also. Does not diversity and inter-mixing help to strengthen the collective human vibration in a positive way?

Yes, it does. For you are all but the same, but society can install this division and in this deepen the route of separation. For if this was not so, their structures would fall instantly. They would have no grounds, for they are all built upon the shaky foundations of identity of separation. For if you are all just in conversation to one thing - to yourself - then are you not only trying to point out that I am right, and I am also wrong? It is pure madness - it is a disease of mind, of your vibrational signature. ABE.

39. We need to bring the sense of the sacred back into our lives. The sense of enchantment and cosmic communion. How can we realize this amongst humanity?

First, recognize your humanity. For when you realize what you truly are, you are humbled. For in the opening up to that of which you are, you realize one thing - that all is the same. There is deep unification in this being - feel right back to this, right back to the core; back to the essence: the life that flows through your veins, the love that opens your heart, the ever-growing knowledge of existence that pulsates and opens up the vibrational signature to so much more. In seeing this unification, you will not be able to restrict your being again. To see that in which it once was, growth is inevitable and in this humanity is taking a big conscious step forward into a new world. A new way, fearless and open to life. ABE.

40. It is said that modern life is making us more isolated and more tribal despite our increased connections. How can we change this situation?

We see that you are not to go back in time to a set of isolated communities but a whole network. This is much like the worldwide web but in physicality - a united network of communication all over the planet and this will then expand. One could liken it to say your individual brains creating another unified brain being that of the planet - then of being of the cosmos. The neural pathways are created by vibrational resonance, and so within is also that without. Is this of understanding now?

41. Talking of alternative communities - will it not be vital to find alternative means of localized energy? Do you envision communities moving

away from global-grid energy supplies? Isn't this a necessity?

Yes, this is what the work of the community is to be - to become self-sufficient. Clearly, not everyone at the start will envision this. But once they come back to unity, when they are less splintered, hear that we say, for it will be an ongoing evolution like everything else. But being amongst and working together in these communities will only strengthen that in which you truly know - that all is but one. When you see that this way of living can only allow you to thrive, then more and more will join in this new way of being. There are such better ways to harvest your energy on this planet and these communities will do so. They will lead the way in new ways, not only working more in harmony but bringing you back to life - to be able to feel and embrace it again. Finally, you will breathe again. ABE.

42. Alternative communities have existed in the past, and some still do today. Yet many have been corrupted by greed, egos, power, etc. Can you say more about how you would envision correct relations to exist within and between balanced communities.

It always will have to come back to this for you to go forward - it is like being lost on a path trying to find the way out then someone will come along and forget also within the distraction of actually being lost. What you have to do is come back to this, knowing first and foremost, otherwise you are but running around in a panic as to what to do and where to go. Stop, realign and readjust. Now, how we envision you to but go about your relations with another; well, that would never be of us to say. For you need to do so this first and then see how it feels; for in this knowing it will be of natural essence to connect. You see, you have but hid yourselves away and gone within - it is but time now to shine, quietly whispering to the ones whom are lost 'I think I know a way out.' ABE.

43. There are some communities who prefer the 'simple life' – living sustainably, sometimes with minimal or no technology, living close to the earth. Many of these are good, honest people who prefer to live away from the noise and distractions. Do you feel these communities will grow in popularity? Are these good examples of how to live in today's cluttered and distracting world?

We just said previously that you are but hidden from the world and we see that it has been of benefit. And like we say about the guru on the top of the hill, we would like it to be seen that you share and communicate and interact and but be in life with the new skills and the new ways and ideas. To share this in which you have learnt whilst taking the necessary time to disconnect - not a shouting off the rooftops or preaching but of a whisper to the ones who want but something else, something real. Is this of understanding? See this, implement the what you call the worldwide web in reality, make these vibrational contacts, these new pathways. ABE.

We so but want to say also it is not a bad thing to go off and disconnect so long as you at some point come back online. You see this?

SECTION FOUR - Science & Technology

Hello ABE and thank you for the continued connection. We appreciate this communication. Now we would like to ask you questions concerning the themes of science and technology.

1. Our science says that our known material universe began with an event they call 'The Big Bang.' How accurate is that? How was the universe created?

Good morning. We are also delighted to have this continued communication. Ah, the big bang - a starting point at which all came into creation. Let me ask you, do you see existence in such a way that there had to be a point of attraction at where it all began? For if all is of one thing then where can you possibly pinpoint a certain point at which it all began? We understand that science has come to this conclusion as they want to see a prominent starting point, but they are also forgetting that what would actually cause this big bang. See it as this, there is vibration, call it a sound, and there are instruments now to receive this vibration and interpret it in any way as such as the mechanism is built. You see, to have a big bang there had to be some sort of starting point at which all came into creation and although this is true in a sense for your physical world it is not true in a vibrational sense and that in what you truly are. See, if you want to get down to the nitty gritty and see the tiny details then you will honestly see that there is space and nothing and within this nothing there is everything and you see that you come from nothing, you play in a world of everything, and then you return to nothing. We are by no means saying that the big bang did not happen and created worlds, but you see it is not the beginning and there will never be a neat little packaged end for this timeline - that you do so hold onto in your physical existence is not so but a circle, a constant becoming. ABE.

2. Our scientists talk about the visible universe, yet the cosmos is a harmonious and complex system larger than the visible universe. Can you say something about the cosmos and its processes of creation?

Yes, we can. It is one of connection, of interaction and, like you say, harmonious interrelationships of this one vibration, being transformed into worlds and living beings and stars and planets. You are able to feel love from outside of yourself but all this time just this one thing, this one vibration, spread out experiencing all things across all created timelines and structures and languages. For in this oneness there is everything and although it looks like nothing in a physical sense it contains it all. You see, at the beginning - and we use this term very, very loosely but so that you can see that in which we want to get across - if in your sciences now you can grasp that beyond even energy it is vibration. That this is source, that this vibration was the beginning of it all. You see, there was never a big bang in a sense for there were no ears to hear that it was; but of itself, like something that turned itself inside out to allow these things to spill from it. For you see, vibration is of nothing - can you grasp it? You can certainly feel it for you have this physical body to sense in such a way, but you cannot hold it and you will never contain it. The more it spreads, the more it creates and interacts and connects and changes. But see this, it is all but one thing - one truth, one vibration, and you are it. ABE.

3. When we say that other universes exist within other dimensions, are we saying that they exist within a different vibrational state? How do multiverses form, and how do they relate?

It is so this way. Multidimensional is just a term for multi vibrations in which you are incapable of experiencing for in your physical existence you have this point. But see this, you are in a sea of vibratory communication; your body would be over stimulated and burn out quickly if it could sense this all at the same time. This is why evolution is key. It is a slowing down of what you already are - like a fine wine to be sipped and enjoyed and revelled in - to be fully immersed in the experience. Does this answer your question?

4. If we could shift our vibrational resonance would we be able to gain access to other multi-vibrational realities?

Yes. But see this, it will not flood in; more so, a revealing of the pathway - so long as you can keep taking vibrational steps forward, in trust of that which will come before you. Is this of understanding now?

5. Our science now agrees on the theory of quantum energy. The quantum plenum, or zero state, is said to be the formless energy field from which the universe manifests. Isn't this quantum zero state also ABE?

It is so this way. But hear this - it is also you.

6. If we are also a part of this zero-state then we have access to incredible energy. How may we manifest this energy - and is this part of our inform function?

You are able to harness this energy as you evolve, and you evolve by allowing this energy also. It is a transactional interaction, for the energy always has to be equal to the mechanism. It is just this so, for if you draw in too much you will blow the fuse so to speak. ABE.

7. Quantum science appears to be the science of the future and understanding of quantum field effects may revolutionize evolution on this planet. What can you say about this?

The quantum field too is best understood as the zero state, or nothing, for you can get into the idea that all is born from this one something. It is not so - it is a resting point at which all is ready to go again and again. Not for reason, for this wave does not have purpose - it expands and interacts and changes form and no form. It is born and it does but is never not there for even when the heart stops beating there is a flatline, a resting point is there not? It is a waving, a peak and trough, a high and a low, around and about, and all this time a dance of polarities is really just the dance of one. Do you see this?

8. Is then the quantum field different from the 'ABE' zero-state? Our science says that all energy is contained in this quantum state. Yet it is also at rest. Could you clarify more on what we call the 'quantum'?

No, it is not. For if all is one, how can it be so. It is where you say it is resting point - it is where form is called one. You could liken it to the state of drawing

things out of a blind bag, like you are pulling something out of thin air, but this is not true for there is
never space and as you evolve you will see this more
and more. For you never just pull something from thin
air but from an all-inclusive pool of consciousness.
Call it quantum, call it ABE, call it you - for all of these
answers will be correct. ABE.

**9. The known universe is said to be held together
by dark energy, and yet our sciences known very
little about this. Could you explain dark energy
and its significance?**

It is a term we like to call a place at which things cannot
be measured for this is the zero state; and although we
say about the quantum field this is but too the same
thing. It is not different; it has a term for science have
been able to call it something for it is the point or cusp
of creation. Now see this, a tube that can stretch out,
circle around back upon itself, all but the same one
tube but points of just the same thing - the tube. Is this
of understanding?

**10. Are you saying that dark energy, zero-state,
and ABE are all the same thing – the same state?**

Yes. For what is in darkness is just but that which has
not seen the light - that being of perception, of the interaction, the splitting apart. Is this of understanding?

11. What are the functions of black holes?

Black holes are just points of different vibratory connections. See this, like the workings of the brain it is necessary for your brain to evolve to make certain neural pathways, connections. This is but so the same for black holes. Is this understood?

12. Could you explain a little more about how black holes function in the cosmos?

Black holes are but the connectors, the points at which when vibrationally aligned will open to reveal a connection, a joining up. See, these pathways are being created within so will then be created without too, to reveal more when the vibrational alignment is connected. When points are joined up, like within the brain, you create a different perception - do you not? Well, this is so for black holes - same thing but outside of yourselves. See, in the resonation you open up **more, creating more pathways, until it all just comes back to one. Is this of understanding?**

13. The galactic core is said to be an 'engine of energy' – how does this energy affect cosmic evolution?

The galactic core is but the inside of the outside. It is but the centre, but also the very outer. It is not really an effect on cosmic evolution but a part of it. You see, in this world of polarity you have to see a grinder and engine room but is not so. It could very well be a large attraction point like, but you see all is attraction, inter-relational. It is things even beyond this that are keeping it in point of attraction. Your science looks on expandment and should rather be looking at vibration, which is in essence nothing, but understand this you are then of understanding of all and the interrelationship of things. We would like to say one thing that these too are gateways - not for other places but for larger and larger connections vibrationally to be made; a piecing together if you will. ABE.

14. Much has been said about the 'galactic alignment' – is this an important phenomenon and how would it affect processes on this planet?

Yes - you see, the pathways are being carved out; they are of a vibrational essence. All the points are there to make these connections. We say but one thing and it is this - a web of consciousness infinitely expanding. Is this of understanding?

15. Do certain galactic/cosmic alignments have an effect on human consciousness? Do such alignments form a part of the process of planetary evolution?

It is so, for it creates a shift; and in that shift you then create a shift and then back and forth and around and around. You see, it is all communicating vibrationally, and always has. You see, there is a conversation that has been going on - all you have to do is allow and listen. ABE.

16. The scientist-inventor Nikola Tesla knew about the energies of vibration. Was he accessing the unified field? Could you comment upon the work of Nikola Tesla?

He was but a person that was open, that could understand particularly vibration - although has been recently more understood - and was taking this infinite power that everyone is capable of. You see, the people who seem to be ahead of their times are usually seen as crazy for they have allowed this energy to flow forth and in this made the necessary connections. They have evolved, you see, in allowing this you enable it and when you enable it you allow it to manifest in physical form. You are making a necessary connection, and in this evolving. But you must see that this connection is but never lost; it's just that you are on but a different frequency. You are blocking it out; you are of material frequency and life wants to cause you to allow cosmic frequency. Is this of a sufficient answer to this?

17. You said that 'life wants to cause you to allow cosmic frequency' – is this then how we develop and evolve, by allowing cosmic frequency to manifest through us and upon the planet?

It is so. But hear this, you are but never apart from it. You are but blocking it out and shutting it down for you do not understand that part of yourselves; and some who do, have over-conceptualised and tied down something that so just wants to flow. You see, you can still be you – 'you' just have to rhythm up, get in tune, by stopping and listening. ABE.

18. To clarify on the functioning of black holes - you said that they operate like inside of a brain, as if creating new neural pathways. Would black holes be like cosmic synapses, creating pathways to stars and aligning with them vibrationally and energetically?

This is exactly so: like one giant brain, one giant consciousness - all but one thing making its way back to this. ABE.

19. There are many irregularities concerning Earth's moon. Some theories speculate that our planet's moon is an artificial structure. Also, that there are other artificial moons/structures in our solar system. Could you comment on this?

Good morning. Ah, the moon as an artificial structure. If we are completely honest, and we want this communication to always be so, then we would say it is nonsense. There will always be theories, for words are just thoughts and everyone is entitled to their own view. But see here, the world was flat until you found the necessary items to connect up and communicate and interact better with your world, and in this discovering yourselves. For it is always inter-relational and you can only discover and connect the points when the two points are at resonation to one another and vibration is the key to creating these cosmic neural pathways - as within, so without. ABE.

20. Although humans reportedly landed on the moon in 1969, there has been no further manned exploration of the solar system. Could you comment on this?

As we said above, the points of connection have to resonate. But see that they are really not apart at all; it is only apart because of the dissonance between them. It is not because you are separated at all; it is that there is a clouding - a mist, a fog, an engaged line or fault on the line would be a better term - that does not enable you to connect and receive. We keep going back to this. But the brain, as you get older and experience more through life, new pathways are created. This is the same with cosmic pathways - the more you allow the more you see. It is always equal in resonance, and discovering your vibratory essence is key to this shift in consciousness which in turn will create more pathways. It is so tightly interwoven. Is this of understanding? We would like to add that there has not been more exploration for you are shifting as a species and maybe just maybe it is time to discover yourselves fully before you could and would be able to create new pathways. ABE.

21. There has been talk recently of attempting to colonize Mars. Is this a positive – or necessary - move forward for our species evolution? Is our species ready to move off Earth?

We do not feel that it is time to do this yet. As we say, we would see it be for this: to benefit the cosmos at all you would really as a whole species have connected more - united within and without. For you see, if you are to do this at present then are you not just bringing more dissonance? We do not feel it is the right time, for you need to discover all that you are and piece it back together. For if as a species you are wanting this colonization from a splintered mind then this will not enable you to move forward. This step, we feel, should always come from a place of unification for it to be of any use or benefit to your species. Love and Light – ABE. We would like to add that just like the brain, the pathways, the connections have to be clear. In this, meaning vibratory flow within is of utmost importance. Is this of understanding?

22. Yes, it makes sense that a species should not consider further colonization in the cosmos until it is unified within. Is this the same understanding with other intelligent species in the cosmos? There is speculation here that other cosmic

species may wish to do us harm - that is, they are in dissonance and not in harmony or unity. Could you comment?

It is not the other species at all, not the ones that are further along evolved, for they could of only evolve by seeing this unification. For in the seeing of this is the way you move forward, you evolve. We would be more inclined to say that a species that is splintered would do far more harm. ABE.

23. In terms of species evolution, there can only be a continued development when there is a recognition of unification and a unified mind. Any species which would wish to cause dissonance would be less evolved. Is this correct?

Yes, this is so. But you see, if your very planet is but evolving too then you will have to shift, or you will not be of resonance. This meaning you have to take the jump at some point from a crumbling tower. ABE.

24. You talk about new 'cosmic pathways' opening up as we make the resonating connections. Is this a way of saying that the cosmos - or further 'unknowns' - will make themselves available to us when we show, as a species, that we are ready? If you like, we could say that we create our own quarantine until we can prove we are ready to move out?

You will always create tighter and tighter restrictions when you are of dissonance, of resistance - it is always so. You create your own little boxes through fear of loss of control, but this needs to be loosened now. You as a species have to see this unification, firstly piecing yourself back together - taking back what society has told you and the way in which you have been conditioned. In turn, this will allow you to allow new connections. Your circles will get larger and expansion will come naturally. But it will only ever be from this place of unification. Why make your life harder by forcing pathways when by allowing would be not only easier but more harmonious? ABE.

25. You stated before that the human body will merge with technology that will result in longer life spans. This issue of the human-cyborg is very controversial. Is this biology-technology merger a natural flow in the evolutionary process? Can you talk more on this?

It will be a natural flow and would be beneficial if it is coming from these unforced pathways of evolutionary connection. We are not asking you to sit around and wait. But firstly, know all that you are for if you can really grasp this as a whole species it will surely be a quantum leap for you in evolutionary terms. ABE.

26. Human scientists are experimenting more with biotechnology, such as DNA modification

**and gene sequencing. There is the probability
here of modifying the human body. This is controversial for many people. Is this an inevitable
part of our species evolution?**

We would like to say too that if, and always, it is
coming from a place of unification. For the splintered
human is just that – splintered. For if you only had
part of the ingredients to make a cake it would not
work, it would not be complete; and in this would
it even be a cake? You see, there is great intention of
making the cake but if you do not have the complete
ingredients to make it then you may well end up with
something that was not intentional at all. Is this of
understanding? The grounding - the unified human -
is one to carve greatness into the world; especially into
a world that is so splintered. But there is great hope,
for all across the planet unification is appearing even
in the darkest corners. ABE.

**27. Technology is advancing at a rapid pace.
We are at a crossroads of where biological life
is merging with technology. Some people are
calling this a new 'post-human' era. Is it a normal evolutionary drive to replace carbon-based
life-forms with technology-machine intelligence?
What can you say about this?**

It is not, no. More so, we would like to say as to support
the biological functioning if need be. But we see that
the way in which you are going is not from a place of

unification - of knowing of this vibrational essence to everything. You really cannot delay this any longer for your species is on the cusp of moving forward. This is why we have continued to manifest, to say 'hold on – let's get this part right first and then when we truly understand this, then we can move forward.' We are not saying that you should listen to us at all but listen and feel to yourselves. Understand yourselves first and foremost before you take a step forward - from a place of love and understanding and not from a place as to which to be a winner of the race. ABE.

28. We agree that our species evolution should not be a race or competition. Yet it seems as if there is another race between the evolution of our awareness about our unitary essence and technological development. If our awareness does not advance sufficiently, doesn't this indicate for problematic futures?

They can only do so if you are not wise, if you are asleep to it. If you don't play the game, then there is no game to play - is it not true? You see, it will cause dissonance for if there is dissonance within then surely it be shown in your very existence and in all you do. Harmonize within and see that this will shine out. You see, when you have a light it cancels out the darkness. It does not eradicate it, but light is shone upon what was only once unseen. We are not saying you should be a perfect species, for there is no such ideal, but to know truly and understand truly without a doubt that in which you are. It is not so to say all should listen and lord this information over each and every one of you. No, but to awaken that little spark to nudge the heart as if to say, 'life is here, it is waiting.' That is all we can ever wish to do. The rest is really up to yourselves. ABE.

We would also like to say that this should never be preached or say that we are right, that this is truth. But to allow you to feel these words in the center of your very being for you to know that what we speak of as truth.

29. Have there been other planets that passed through an advanced technological evolution? If so, how did they experience this process?

There is, and there have – yes. Every planet is differing in its needs of these differing technological advancements. But see this, it is all to be used and only to enhance the organism. So be very wary if your species is using these in ways to control and manipulate, for they are not the purpose for someone who is coming from a place of unification at all. We have seen this battle before, but it can be overcome by knowing that in which you are - knowing your power and place of resonance. Controlling and manipulation will always try to push forth. In some sense, it is in the knowing of what you are is where your power really lies. ABE.

30. There are international efforts to develop forms of artificial intelligence. This could be incredibly positive for the evolution of human civilization or highly problematic. What can you say about artificial intelligence?

Again, we feel like a stuck record; but this is only truth. It needs to be from this place of unification always. We see that there are people in power and who have the money and resources to do this now who one could say is not of unification and are very much in it for the race. But you see, you always think that you are powered by such people when in reality it is the other way around. The masses are awakening to this disso- nance - they are claiming back their power. Artificial intelligence will be of benefit if, like we say, it is a tool, an enhancement to the lives of others. Otherwise, it is of no use for it will be in the wrong hands. ABE.

We are by no means saying that this transition to unifi- cation will be a complete easy ride, for there will be destruction and dismantling of old structures. But see this, it is making way for these new connections that have unified within and therefore can only unify without, claiming back your evolutionary stance. ABE.

31. With increased automation of our lives more and more people will be compelled to find answers for the role and function of the human being. How can people seek for meaning in an increasingly controlled world?

Meaning is always that in which you make it, always. It is never outside of you. You have been conditioned in such a way that this is always sought outside of yourselves, but it is not so. One can find meaning in the seemingly mundane where others it is doing great. What we would like to say that all meaning is, is really just connection. Like the universe wants to know itself through itself, so this is true for you. Connect, be open, be true. ABE.

32. Powerful technologies – such as cyber and bio-technologies – are increasingly in the hands of small groups or even individuals. Will this create a dissonance of power relations that could create greater uncertainty amongst humanity?

If people are wise to what they are; if they stand strong in the knowing of this unification, then they would not even entertain the game at all. It is only when you are splintered that you are powerless. There will be a struggle of power between people claiming theirs back and the few who remain to want to manipulate and control. And they will do so through fear, but the harmonization of such will balance out. We are never claiming of what your species see as all good - this is a world of polarity. But bringing back to balance is key - centering yourselves first. ABE.

33. Virtual/Augmented reality and video games are increasingly popular amongst the young people. These interactions also have the capacity to re-wire our brains, do they not? Some people are worried about young people's fixation with such activities. Could you comment on this?

Yes, it does but re-wire and re-adjust. It is about balance. But see this, they are of understanding that this is so a game - for the ones that are of entrapment are really the ones stuck in a reality and are unaware that they are but playing a game at all. Is this of understanding?

34. What advice could you give us about the development and use of technologies?

The only advice we would like to give is use them to enhance life and be very wary if a technological advancement creates dissonance rather than connection, for this will only be moving you away further from the truth, enabling the few to keep this power and redeeming you as powerless. All technological advancement, if more and more become unified, will enable you to explore yourselves, your world, and the cosmos more. And in this waking up, more and more people creating greater and greater neural pathways within and without in the cosmos. This will, of course, need your species to evolve, to advance in some way. But always it should be of promoting connection and pathways. ABE.

We would also like to add, if you are prompting us to state what technological advancements will occur, then we would like to say that we are understanding that technology is advancing at a rapid pace and it seems to be very much still in the hands of the few who may use such technologies to create dissonance. More so, what we have to say is that it will only be balanced out again or taken back if people are wise to it - not everyone, for like a wave it will spread anyway. But for these new pathways to be formed there has to be that first step - that first one or few who will walk it first and say, 'look, it is not so scary as you think.' Do you understand why we talk so much about getting this key foundation set first? We leave you now with much love and light and great gratitude to be able to come forth. ABE.

35. Life extension is now a major research area. Some scientists wish to eradicate death. This sounds good, but is it wise to try to eliminate the natural dying of our bodies? This could be problematic for vibrational signatures as well as over-population. Could you comment on this?

It will always be of your sciences and technological establishments that want to eradicate the natural processes of life. And although it is seen as a good thing to prolong life, we do so feel it should be more of a natural process. But hear this, we are not at all discounting your advancement as a species, and although life expectancy will be prolonged due to technological advancements and the morphing of biological and technical, we do so feel that in a biological sense it should still be of a natural process. It is also so that you are changing in form with these new vibrations, so there will also be a natural evolutionary process to your being. But as we see it, you cannot rush this process too far forward. Of course, you can push the boundaries of life, but what we want to say is that it must always take in this whole picture. Now, we understand that you would very much like to prolong your experience in physical form. But we also see the need not to meddle in it too much, for you will upset the natural rhythm if pushed too far and that could be catastrophic. For not only you but to that of the whole cosmos. You see that there is a fine line between enhancing and completely dominating, controlling, and forcing life for all life is a balancing act and really you must see this place of unification as we see it. To advance much more balanced, much more smarter and much more in flow, trying not to cause further dissonance. ABE.

36. Following on from the above, there was a news report released today stating that birth rates had radically fallen in the last half a century. Perhaps natural processes will adjust for such things as population and we don't need to try to overtly socially manage this?

It is true that you do need to take a step back at some point to allow balance to appear. Now see this, balance can look destructive and chaotic like things are far from balance for your social constructs have built their buildings upon changeable foundations. You see that you as humans in your own lives, for example, you do not know when things will change and take a different course. You see, life has this funny way of changing direction within a heartbeat - come back to yourself, feel back into your bodies. Bring all those vibrational attachments back in and just see even if for just a moment in this deep rest. Even if just momentarily, you will have a deep sense of the world and your part within it. You will see that there is a time for doing and there is a time to sit and just watch the grass grow. ABE.

37. Time, as we measure it, is a linear path, based on solar movement and planetary effects. Understandably, time as we experience it is a local phenomenon. Yet there is also much speculation on the science of time-travel. Could you say something about how 'time' is experienced or recognized throughout the cosmos?

It is very much of linear process, yes, in your physical existence. For in a sense, it is in harmony for you at this stage in time in your evolutionary process. You see time as around and around on your clocks, but as a line of points at to which can be recorded too. Now, which one could it be? That time is of a circular pattern re- repeating itself, or could it be a long line in which things appear upon and are recorded and dated? But you come to know that time is only but a social construct; to say, I was here and I can prove it because, you see, I existed from one time to another. It was really a mere measurement of existence of individual things at differing times. Now, what we say is if you took away your clocks and your timelines for a mere moment you would see that it is only here, now. And although we do not like the concept of 'now,' for it has been over-used, it is but a statement of continuous becoming, and you are never apart from it. The functionings of your vibrational signature allow you to ponder upon the future by thinking about the past. But you see, you are here with it - there is nowhere to get to so long as you can see that and not be attached to future or longing for past. That you are merely here with life and able to do these wondrous things within this time-space reality. You see, we are never here to say 'be here' for it is a wondrous gift to be able to think of the future and mull over past experience - that is being human and being of physical form. It is the attachment to race ahead or drag yourselves back to what once was. You see that there is no time, just a becoming and to state that there is a now and you should be in it is also a false premise, a past - for the moment you try to become present it has already passed, has it not? Throughout the whole of the cosmos you experience time differently. Some, no time at all; just an interaction of being. And some that have made these new pathways through evolutionary process and vibrational connection to allow them to jump time – time, in regards to your measurement - of the one thing, the one happening, the one constant and infinite becoming. ABE.

38. As we shift into a new phase of human civilization we will require new forms of energy extraction and distribution. Scientists are working hard on nuclear fusion/fission, hydrogen power, and similar forms that use atomic elements. Yet is there a way to utilize the quantum or zero energy to provide for our needs? Isn't it time that we understood how to access new energy forms that are cosmic rather than planetary?

It is, and you will step into this process only when you are of full understanding of vibration and unification. There is infinite power in this source of zero state. But you see, you can harness this for yourselves for this too is of you and from the world around. No longer will you have to rely upon physical material sources to power your world, but to look to vibrational attraction for this is the key that holds much power. But hear this, you must also firstly - and this is of great importance - come to this place of unification for this power could be used for destruction rather than benefiting yourselves as a species. Is this of understanding now?

39.Are we likely to discover and utilize a science of vibrations within this century? Where will science go from here? What can we expect next?

Science is moving forward, and they are becoming more and more so aware of the unseen and even the unmeasurable. But hear this, they have not yet fully unified this, for they are still very much separate things. When science can see the vibrational element is really no differing from that of your physical existence it will go much further. It will make these pathways, these neural pathways, clear to join up. If they could firstly join up matter and vibration, well, science will excel and in this will cause you to join up the dots within. We cannot say a specific time for it is all about the allowance of this connection which is trying to pave a new path. We see that it will be of great significance over the next 10 years or so in the discovery of moving forward to a more unified existence, and in this an emergence of one could say spirit and matter. But hear this, when science knows undoubtedly that these two things were never of separation at all - that there was merely a fault on the line, a contamination of sorts – well, it will be of fast movement forwards. Of infinite expansion of mind, a more cosmic communicative system. For you see, in the move forward your brain expands; it creates new pathways and in this you create this within the cosmos too. And with this you become more of a communicative race without the need of material substance. Is this of understanding?

40. Some popular scientists are publishing books about how to create colonies on other planets and interstellar travel, etc. They say this is the future of humanity. Are they preparing the human species in advance? Or is this misconceived belief and a result of the splintered mind?

We would like to say it is of advancement, but we see so much that there is very much still this splintered mind. See this, an allowance of vibration to a splintered mind, the flow, is there - it can never not be. But it is but falling upon an object that will split apart and not fully understand this unification. Now, if you were to allow and also understand unification it will flow through the process. You would be the channel that brings connections rather than the one that allows, and then sifts, and sorts, and places through your own vibrational signature. And although we always say that it is not to be rid of it, is in the knowing of when to put it aside and to be of service to yourself, and in this to the whole. Is this of understanding?

41. Our science still believes that space travel will be accomplished by forms of energy propulsion. Is it not more probable that humanity will explore the cosmos through extended consciousness rather than physical bodies?

We do so see this, yes, for now. But it will be of sorts to come that you will not need apparatus to visit, for your bodies will be differing. See it like this, you hear of near-death experiences to be that some see God or enter heaven and see loved ones. This is but the vibrational signature not leaving the body. For we do not see start and end, or that of a soul. This is why we use vibrational signature for it is what one would call mind too. They have these experiences for even though the body is dead the consciousness is not so. The vibrational signature is back into the zero state although never being apart - it just does not have the channel in which to express through. It is into this cosmic consciousness, if you will, just a different state. The reason that people can remember this and although being clinically dead in your material existence, there is a point in which vibrational alignment or resonance is still to that of this body and its conditionings. We understand that this may of gone off of the question quite a bit, but what we are really trying to express is that the more pathways that are created through you, and then within the cosmos, the less need there will be to explore in a physical sense for you will see that consciousness is but free to travel and is not as constrained as you once thought so. ABE.

42. The advancement of computation has given us the perspective that the cosmos operates similar to a kind of program. Some people speculate that we are living inside of a grand cosmic computer program and that our lives are like a simulation. Would this be a suitable analogy?

We would rather but see it more so as an evolutionary process, more so a brain. You see, we talk about these neural pathways and we mean that for both on the material level and also that of the cosmos level. Is this of understanding? For you see, if there is just one thing and you are it, then what is within is also without on a larger scale - a going back if you will to the Russian doll analogy. ABE.

43. Many people now experience synchronicities in their lives, and 'signs' as if - they say - the 'universe' is speaking to them. Are there such interventions where messages are placed into the material realm?

Not so much a placement but of an allowance. But you see, you have to be aware of them too. But hear this, some people get so caught up in the signs and synchronicities they grab a hold of them - as in a way to know and therefore control or resist certain experience. You see, there is always a knowing of sorts if you are allowing; and allowing is knowing. And then in this the universe is then always in communication with you. ABE.

44. New technologies are likely to be more accessible to the elites - especially such things as genetic enhancement. Isn't there a possibility that the human race will be divided by this rather than unified?

It is so a possibility. But you see, are you not then putting continued power to those at the top so to speak? You see, they are interested in power and at present power is money. This will shift course, and of course there will be someone who will want to manipulate whatever commodity is of utmost importance for your survival as a species. You will see that in the shifting of yourselves there will be a shifting of power. It will be placed back into the hands of the many rather than the few. But hear this, it will be a struggle for you have allowed it for such a long time and have left many things dormant and gathering dust. It is not a battle of power as such; more so, a shift. Is this of understanding? We would also like to add that a unified being is of utmost importance now for this is where you will gain all your power back - all your pieces that have been splintered for so long. Yes, there will be technological advancements and no doubt be people that will want to control and manipulate. With this we are not stating a euphoric existence but a real one. But you see, the more and more people that are understanding and knowing of this unification, this vibration in which you are being shifted to resonate with, to understand, the more these structures will not be able to withhold. For you see, the animals that became extinct were the ones that could not resonate to their systems; and therefore, could not continue into the new vibrational evolution. Is this of understanding now?

45. To bring back power to the masses, we need to shift our vibrationary state – to drop our social conditionings, our ego, our fixed identities, and to allow a connection for consciousness to flow. If people can resonate to a new state of being, then so will our social systems shift and evolve. Is this what you are saying?

Yes, this is true. But see, these things do not have to be dropped permanently and cannot. One could liken it to a good clear-out of such, then put back once you have given the shelving a good dusting. Is this of understanding?

46. It seems obvious that technology is now a permanent part of our human lives. At the same time there will be a need to be closer to Nature - maybe a wish to return to more agrarian lifestyles. How can this seeming contradiction between high technology and pastoral living be balanced?

It can be used to harness this zero-state - this vibrational attraction - for it can power your life in such a way that there will be no need to rip apart your world to create more power. It will also be in such a way that your own being is the power point and there will be no need for others to control and manipulate. For how could one manipulate if all you need is all you have right now? In this it will create more of a unified field of communication, not only in your physical existence but that of the cosmos too. ABE.

47. Scientists have constructed a complex parti-cle accelerator – the Hadron collider – to search for new particles and to examine unsolved ques-tions in physics. Some people view these exper-iments as risky. Is this a wise way to operate in order to know the cosmos better?

You see, there will always be things that come up for you to scrutinize and pinpoint a point of your exis-tence. It is done so in a way to utilize power; to create points at which this power can be utilized. Which way that seems to go is unclear. For as we like to say, a splintered mind/being is far more likely to use this for their own gains rather than using it for a more unified purpose. We see that scientists are getting the focus to smaller and smaller particles to enable them to figure out your material existence. But see this, the more and more focused it becomes the more it is pinpointed, the more splintered your existence becomes. Open up and you will see the greatest power source and in this you will discover yourselves. We are not saying that you should not become focused on the details but firstly you need to open up, then to re-adjust. ABE.

48. Scientists note that our local galaxy – which we call the Milky Way – contains around a billion planets that are 'Earthlike' in their properties. Our strongest telescope can spot about 100 million galaxies in the visible universe. In an earlier communication you stated that there are only 5 planets in the cosmos, including ours, that is at an advanced stage of evolution. Isn't this a small number compared to the potentials?

It is. But see this, there are more that harbor life in a different way. What we are saying is that there is only a small amount that are in relation to your type of physicality of being. This is not to mean that you are a minority. Far from that, but a small part of differing life spread across all of the cosmos. You see, it is only now as technology has evolved that you are discovering what has been in your deepest oceans for millennia. Is this of understanding?

49. Contact with other advanced intelligences, say our scientists, is more likely to come from powerful electronic brains rather than humanoid, biological species. How close is this to the truth?

We would like to say that it is not so, for you always have that in which you need. See this, you are always receiving; you are never apart from this. It is only in your vibrational signature that is contaminating connection in a way. But you see, it would not serve you either to be rid of it. It is always about the whole, the unification of things. If you can really get to grips with this, then there will be no limits. But you see, you have been contaminated with the notion that you are a physical being and even though this is so there is much more to you than that. It is in the resonance of allowing your being to accept and allow new forms, new pathways, new ways of communication. If you do not understand this unification, then it will not serve you to open up; for it will cause dissonance of vibrations in which you hold. Is this of understanding?

50. How can we build up, or develop, our means on communication with the cosmos and other non-terrestrial intelligences?

Trust in what you are, knowing of this unified system, allowing vibrational resonance, allowing open heart communication. But see this, before you are to try this be sure for it to be firmly rooted into your being, into all that you do on this level first. ABE.

51. Science sees physical evolution on the earth as related to environmental factors, including phases of glaciation. But are not phases of con-

sciousness 'directed' and managed as evolutionary impulses upon the earth?

You see, the Earth evolves in physicality and then the species upon that planet have no choice but to move with it. You see, your planet is evolving, and you are doing so in unison. See it like this, you are at a place of work and they put in a new technological advancement to help be more productive. They get rid of the old system and install a new one. Now the workers will have to adapt, will have to learn new ways of being. If not, they could be let go of for they will not be beneficial to the whole operation. Is this of understanding? We are not trying to denounce your part as human beings for it is a true gift. But we are merely trying to put forth that when your planet shifts you have no other choice but to shift with it and this goes further and further out until zero state again, and back around and re-creating and changing form and no form. It is so tightly intertwined but always at the core is pure consciousness, just reflecting and retracting and shifting and dancing. Is this of understanding?

52. Are you saying that past human species went extinct because they were unable to adjust to the earth's evolving shifts and resonance?

Yes, this is what we are but saying. For something to grow - and this is such for you as individuals - some things have to be dropped, they cannot go forward on the same paths. Like the seed that wanted to grow so much, it bust apart all that it was and in this had taken on another form. Is this of understanding?

53. Technology is often regarded as referring to mechanical-type devices. Is there not also a 'spiritual technology' whereby we can develop our internal senses. Perhaps even re-wire our brains and nervous system? What would you say about this?

For is not technological, or as you state mechanical type devices, still but an expression of this, of this one thing? For it has come through but the physical organism through consciousness. What makes the complete difference between them is what vibration it is being filtered through - splintered or unified?

54. The science of intention and manifestation is both recognized and yet similarly ignored by many. How is internal intention related to external manifestation in our reality?

It is but a filter of consciousness you can allow what is meant to be for you. For you see, it has been a big thing for so long and has been made such a big fuss of and in this you really have contaminated the line. The pathways have been stopped dead in their tracks. For you have tried to be positive and although it may have its benefits it is very much splintered and much cause of dissonance. We are not saying at all to be passive but unification in oneself is much more a powerful force in the world than a splintered vibration. You can have an intention, you always will for your physical existence. But see this, allow it to come; loosen up the grips of what is meant to be for your very essence knows the path and you have to trust in that. Once more, open up that heart and allow. ABE.

55. We feel that science and technology are focusing too much upon the externals of physical existence, whereby we need now to focus on the intangible, non-physical aspects if we are to successfully develop as a species. Could you comment on this?

It is true, and this is what we mean also in the taking it back to the bare bones. For you are stripping all condition away, which is very much a physical thing, to reach back to this zero-state, and say 'now we're gathering things all back together.' For in this nothing, in this unseen non-physical part of existence, is the key to many leaps forward as a species - and creating new neural pathways within and without. Is this of understanding now?

56. Thank you ABE, for your patience with us. We hope to continue this communication and further allow this understanding. Is there anything else you would wish to communicate before we finish this session?

We are glad to be discussing such things and is well and good to ask these questions for they are of importance and are of depth to communicate well that in which we want to put forth. We do hope that this is to continue, and we see things aligning for next steps to be taken. We wish for you to connect and follow your own guidance for that too is but us and also of you. We would like to say but one thing and that is we really want you to see what a true gift it is to be in physical form and although we try to walk in the middle by neither being overly positive as to delude you of a perfect future, we do not either want to instill fear for this is not our purpose. Our true purpose is to hand it all back - all the constraints that have been put upon you by others and all those that you have put upon yourselves. We hope to continue this communication. ABE.

SECTION FIVE - Humanity & its Future

1. Many people consider humanity to be at a crossroads where a breakthrough or a breakdown is more sensitive. To survive this phase will depend on our state of consciousness and whether we shift quick enough from a splintered to a unified mind? What can you say about this?

Yes, this is but true that evolution is one of conscious unity. See it like this, your consciousness is like the glue that will piece what you really are back together again if you so allowed it. But your vibrational signature but separates and boxes things up. This is due to your social conditioning. You see, it blinkers out this state of being in order to make you a good citizen. Seldom do people allow this into their everyday conscious experience, and in this they have the blinkers on. They do not have the full picture; they do not operate at full capacity and to live a life in such a way - a life that could be so much more - is the greatest shame of your human experience. But see this, you can only have a breakthrough if you have a breakdown of old paradigms; and if old is crumbling then it paves way for new pathways, new connections, and in this breakdown there will be great breakthrough as people will be searching within themselves for something that resonates; something that sticks; something that makes them so feel human again. ABE.

2. What are likely to be the consequences if humanity, as a whole, is unable to recalibrate its balance and resonance with the planet? What timescales are we talking about?

You see, it does not work in such a way for it is in unison - not one to full vibrational capacity, then other; no, but an inter-relational nudging. You see, there is a lot to be said already for vibrational resonance. For people are changing and you can see there is much balance within. The reason for us to come forth is because we see that this resonance is tipping the scales again in a way that people are still engrossed in their own vibrational signatures. For they are understanding this unified field, but they are shifting to make it into something special, something above and beyond, something that you have to aspire to or make yourselves equal to - you have to be better, to not get angry or sad. But you see, this would not be of balance at all and would not be of a human experience. The only way to unity is accepting the light and the dark, the love and the hate, as but the same thing because within this unity you realize that you are perfectly imperfect, and that is wonderful. Is this of understanding? When you ask but of a timescale to this, we would be so inclined to say within the next century. For you see, to really uproot what has been common knowledge, for humanity needs to also be uprooted from the minds of humanity and this will take time for people will feel a gaping hole where what once stood a statue of self, and you had built your whole world around it. But you see, this gap does not need to be filled again but to allow life to flow uninstructed through your being. We would like to strip things back to the name of 'no name' for even after all this communication with us you too will even have to drop us to see this truth also. ABE.

3. We dream about the future. Some people say they can see into the future. Surely the future is a set of potentials rather than a fixed destiny? What can you say about this?

We would be inclined to say that it is but both. Now see this, there are fixed outcomes as an inevitability. For example, you throw an egg at a wall; in its natural state it is going to smash. But there are many differing factors that could be changed in order to give a different outcome if you're consciously aware. Say, for example, you make a target you are more certain as to where that would hit. Or, if you did so boil the egg first it would most probably not smash the egg at all; well, not in the way it would do so as before. Is this of understanding?

4. Humans are dreamers. What happens to our vibrational signature during the sleep state? Do our dreams have significance?

This is but the time that you give up this vibrational signature. You are at resting point and you see you are back to zero state - you are unified. We would rather but see dreaming as waking up for you are so conditioned to be active and doing. We are not saying that this should be such a way for your physical existence, but of unified collaboration, conscious and unconscious - the whole picture. For in this state of being you are allowing and also able to act. You are aware and also allowing - this is resonance of your very being. This is resonance to your planet, and this is resonance to the universe. ABE.

5. Life seems to be so highly complex and yet based upon some very simple laws. What are these laws?

The laws are ————for there are no laws. For the moment you speak you have taken it away from that in which it really is. But we see this may not suffice as good for us to give an explanation of how the world or cosmos works. So, we say this - it is all and will always ever be a vibrational resonance. This is true across all times, all space; and when resonance happens, physicality is created. You have long forgotten your vibrational essence and how it is tying and binding itself to things and places and people and experiences, and future outcomes and past problems. One simple thing;

one thing – vibration. Remember this and you really do remember yourselves. Bring this into your conscious minds and you will see it in all that you interact with. Is this of understanding?

6. We have been told before by other teachings to 'raise our vibration.' It sounds good. Yet it also sounds abstract and New Age. How can we explain to the average person to raise their vibration?

You allow it. Strip it back; all the conditions in which you have put upon life, upon yourselves, and upon others. Give life room to move again within you, for there isn't a state to get to - it is here. It's just that you have the blinkers on, the social blinkers - take those off and allow all that you are. See the unity in all that you do, and your vibration will be nothing but resonance to your world, to each other. In this you will be creating heart-to-heart connections in all that you do. ABE.

7. If a person begins to shift their vibrational resonance, this will affect others in whom they come into contact with – like a transmitter? Isn't this one aspect of how change can manifest, by positively infecting others, so to speak?

You can do so. But see this, if their vibrational essence is one of pure resistance then it will at first not have any flow. But hear this, it is of not forcing at all but of you continuously resonating at that at which you are - and in this it will break through at some point, weathering away at that contamination. The only thing you can do is not allow it to contaminate yours. If so, it is but a good idea to strengthen your own connection before trying to change that of others. Is this of understanding now?

8. The truth of reality is so difficult for our rational, splintered minds to grasp. We wish to understand that we can access connections with the cosmic mind/unified consciousness, yet it seems so far away from our everyday lives. How can we shift into a state of knowing?

You see, like we said before you have been conditioned in such a way to block it out and to hurry up and just get on with it. For this will make you easy to handle, predictable, and safe - but this is not true. In this conditioning you have become more and more disconnected. For a splintered mind creates just that - a splintered world, and in that a splintered cosmos. To move forward you have to understand that this is how it is. That it is all but a unified field - and we are not bad, we are it. In this realization that we are it, in this deep knowing that 'oh yes, its all the same and I am it too,' you let up the character. It is not so important you let yourselves and others off the hook. But see this, it is a process, it is a becoming. Of this there are lots of conditioning to unwrap. Is this of understanding?

To shift into a state of knowing then, you have to be allowing. Your current paradigm is one of resistance to what is not physical and in this you shut out vibration. You shut out yourselves, tightening the conscious experience, restricting it. The only way to allow is to rest. Just for now, gather in all the wires of intention, the hooks of belief - reel them back in just for now and rest. Gather and recalibrate the system – harmonize, unite.

9. There will be many people who will consider it crazy that a 'unified zero state field' called ABE is speaking to them. What would you say to them?

Ahh, yes. It would be so such a way because you have been conditioned in such a way as to shut this out, for it is not of service, to keep order and obedience. But you see, the name is not of importance at all. For like we said, even after this connection and writings - and there will be but plenty more writings - we would say drop it too, for you are allowing zero state to come forth and in this you are allowing all that you are. You are allowing pure consciousness to express in physical form. This is not available to just the few but to each and every one, if they do so allow. Drop it all and allow. Is this of understanding now?

10. Some may say that the age of religion is over. We no longer need the crutches of intermediary teachings when we can access Source direct-

ly. Is humanity moving into an era of conscious communication with Source? Is this necessary to evolve further as a species on this planet?

It is this way, yes. You are but moving into a different pathway, a conscious evolution. It is so that in the loosening of your own individual vibrational signatures you allow more and more of this energy in - this vibration. We do not want you to be rid of your vibrational signature for this will never be so. But you see, in the allowance of the new vibration it shakes loose the contamination that has been considered your vibrational signature for so long. You will harmonize your vibrational signature with that of the zero-state vibrational essence. It will be of resonance, not of riddance. Is this of understanding now?

It is of essence to move forward. But you see, at some point you have to STOP, readjust, and then move forward again from a different place.

11. We've changed our life rhythms. Rather, our new technological environment has altered our rhythms, and we've not had sufficient time biologically, as well as psychologically, to adjust. What would you say about this?

It is true. Technology has created dissonance in such a way that your evolution has been stunted. You see, it has to be that unified nudging, and you have not been inclined to feel that nudge. Now, it has to be more so of a blow rather than a nudge. You see, technological advancement will always serve humanity from its own state of consciousness, and at present it is still very much splintered. To really make it of use you can see from the worldwide web that it is all about connections and widening your communicative scope, your consciousness. Is this of understanding, for you see it is always relational?

We would also like to say but one thing - you see, it is never about ridding life of yourselves: sitting upon a hilltop void of self, void of world, no. But what it is, is to take away the false self that has been socially constructed. Let that go, allow this vibrational essence to flow through your being, birthing a new vibrational signature - a non-splintered one, a unified one. It is almost like taking off the band-aid on a cut, allowing the body to harmonize and heal. This is what we come forth; for not to have no self - although there really is no self - but to allow a more harmonized self. The birthing of a whole new humanity, one consciousness at a time, one vibrational alignment at a time. We are grateful for this communication and will continue as long as need be. ABE.

12. Thank you, ABE. What you say sounds similar to what was said by the Indian mystic Aurobindo. He referred to the 'Supramental' or 'Overmind' and how we need to allow it to manifest through us - to 'bring in' this unified consciousness. What can you say about this?

It is so. A collaboration, as you would say, in your physical existence of minds. But mind is vibrational signature and vibrational signature is caused by the vibrational resonance, to create pathways within the brain. This is exactly what it is like outside of you - like a web of consciousness within it so now needs to be allowed without also. Is this of understanding?

13. So, are you saying that one of the functions of the human being is to collaborate with the unified consciousness, to develop resonance, and allow pathways for a pure consciousness to manifest? That is, to form more pathways of connection and unity?

Yes, it is. It is about widening your field of consciousness - opening up the dolls of being contained within another and another until you see 'but oh yes, I am that and that is but me, I were just encased.' Is this of understanding?

14. Humanity is mapping the world and the cosmos like never before. We are seeking deep into the oceans. We are mapping the entire solar system, and our telescopes search deep into the cosmos. What will we find if we don't first find ourselves?

Nothing. You can only ever but find yourselves. But if so coming from a splintered mind, you are finding everything else but yourselves. Is this of understanding?

15. Many people - from scientists to philosophers – are saying that we are entering a post-human era. How can we be going 'post' human if we haven't yet discovered what being human truly means?

This is why it is of utmost importance to strip it back, figure out this part of yourselves in which has been closed off. In the realization of yourselves you see all that you are and all that you have ever been, and that is the whole thing. And from this point new pathways will be open, new things will be seen, new resonance. But see this, they will be new to the eyes that have not yet been open but old news to those that have been awake. ABE.

16. It can be said that the human is both 'being and becoming' – this seems to suggest a combination between a state of rest and a state of evolving. Is there some truth to this?

Yes. It is always this so - you have to be in tune with what you are to allow these subtle shifts to take course within you and create new horizons outside of you.

17. Can you give some examples when the pure consciousness was manifested upon our planet?

It is always a flow, but I realize you are asking who or what has brought it forth before and we can say that there has been many, and this has always been in relation to that of the pathways that are so created at the time of being. It is really manifested in all that you do. But see this, it is but always dependent upon the pathways within the vibrational signature of how this manifests in your world. This is why we are coming forth - to allow a recalibration, a reset if you will. To harmonize what is available to you at your next evolutionary step of creating vibrational pathways - not only within but without too. Is this of understanding?

18. By recalibrating our resonance and alignment, are we also physically re-wiring connections in our brain? Is this what is meant by our potential for neuro-plasticity?

It is so, yes. You are not only doing so with the brain but also DNA is receiving this new shift, this new alignment. All is in conversation - it just depends upon what conversation it is, and what you are so to allow. ABE.

19. Would this mean that old patterns or neural connections will become obsolete because they are no longer of resonance? If this is so, then this would also cause habit patterns in our lives to be broken down too, wouldn't it?

Yes, this is so. Connections will be lost within and this will also affect your outer lives too. This may look like loss, but it is only opening up for new pathways to be formed which are more of resonation to your being and to that of which is trying to manifest in form. ABE.

20. You have spoken much about humanity's splintered mind. What other things do we need to change or shift in order to better harmonize with our future?

Firstly, this unification of self - that is it. We do not want to give but a long 'to do' list. Just this for now - find this. ABE.

21. The future is a complex subject. We understand you may not wish to disclose too much – yet what can you tell us about humanity's future?

It is always in but relation to that of which you have unified. For the path, for so long, has been one of restriction of consciousness. You are on the other side of becoming a round-about circle, and when but this phase has come once you have readjusted, reset.

You are but setback on becoming. Take, for example, a child riding a bike - you gently direct and readjust for the child can take this or leave it. It is completely up to them and in this it creates the paths. Is this of understanding?

You see, it is very simple; and by labelling and scrutinizing something you then loose the very meaning. It is to be seen, to be watched, to be felt - for in this the secrets of the universe are revealed. And in this you realize that there was never a secret to be found - you just had to allow yourself to fall back into resonance into you. Is this of understanding?

22. You have mentioned about becoming harmonized to what is available to us at our next evolutionary step. Could you explain more what you mean by this?

Yes, but of course. You see, it is really about allowing - like the wave that has a high and a low, a rest and peak. It could be likened of action and inaction; this is allowing resonance. Knowing but when to rest and see, and readjust, before taking off into action. This is but the lower point of the vibrational wave, and to fuss and fight and to have to constantly keep it in a straight line of resonance you are in hindsight flat-lining life. It is a constant balance between the two, and to know when is where you have to re-attune yourselves. Is this of understanding?

You see, there are many belief systems and constructs that tell you to pick a side and stick with it, and life does not move in such a way. Life is a wave of vibrational potential.

23. Following on from what you say about the high and low points of vibrational waves. Does this suggest that currently humanity is at a 'lower point' on the vibrationary wave? That higher energies are coming that will shift this trajectory?

It is to say that. But do not take higher and lower as, to say, in your own constructs, sense of the words, for they are of equal resonance. But yes, you are but in a dip. It is the time to readjust, realign, and then move forth. For if not so, you will continue with this path of resistance and constant action. Is this of understanding?

You see, in the constant path of action you are but killing life. You are straightening it out, and also it goes for the other end of constant rest. It has to be of resonance - of movement, of rest, of breath. ABE.

That energy is always there; it is just that the evolution is one of consciousness now. It always, but always, has to be in resonance to the mechanism or organism that is receiving such vibrations. Is this of understanding?

24. What is the source for this 'dip' in vibrational resonance - is it due to cosmic conditions? Is it

that the organism (humanity) has not evolved in line to receive the vibrations of consciousness - are we in need of a nudge?

It is such this. But also, just local. For like we say, there are at this point contained vibrational waves and dips which are of locality - physical points like the synapses. You see, the vibrational essence or resonance that would connect the two have to be of resonance. The connections cannot and will not be made until your own individual pathways have been readjusted, reset, and reunited. Is this of understanding now?

We are but the nudge. But you are also of that too. ABE.

25. So, until this readjustment and realignment can occur, humanity is, in a sense, 'cut off' from the full cosmic connection and communication. As a species, we need to develop our collective synapse in order to create the pathway, the bridge. Is this a fair description?

It is, yes. At some point you need to stop - gather and rest, readjust, and realign with this wave, this vibration. It is like when you sing too fast in a song and get ahead of yourselves or are too slow and therefore you are still far behind. It is of a mutual emergence. Is this of understanding?

A mirror, a dance of vibrational resonance. ABE.

26. And this readjustment can begin with individuals? Does it require a 'tipping point' - a sufficient mass - rather than a whole species adjustment?

It has to be started there from the beginning. Like we say, back to the barebones of things. For there is but too much noise, too much contamination. Of course, it will always be so - that the more weight in the scale will tip the balance just that tiny bit. What we want to say, that indeed it does not have to be the whole species but a balance of sorts. Is this of understanding?

You see, it will be this way and more and more will follow. Like the cycle we talk of, you're stepping into a dip, whereas the old action orientated resonance is too much - it is going around again to rebalance. But see this, it will always be a kind of tug-of-war to keep balance. For you see, when someone likes a certain food they would want more and more, and in this get tired of it at some point. It will not resonate, so it will go back to zero and rethink about the choices. This can be likened to that of this kind of scenario. Is this of resonance to you? Can you see that in which we speak? For it is always a becoming. ABE.

27. How do you sense this will unfold? Personally, we have a positive view on humanity's future. How does ABE consider the readjustment process, or period?

It will be one of discomfort, for all readjustment is uncomfortable. For if you have been sitting in a certain position for a while, when you come to move to another position it is of discomfort, is it not? But this discomfort remains to be seen as to how tightly you hold on to outdated paradigms and how allowing you are to this vibration. That's why you see it is a time to stop and see. Is this of understanding?

28. Will this discomfort period cover the rest of what we call the 21st century? Or will it be a shorter span? (We realize it is somewhat difficult to talk about time lengths).

You see, this that it is so. But if you are able to tip the balance just a little, we would see this be happening within the next 10 years. But see this, it will be a tug-of-war between what is and what wants to become. And could even see this time shortened, so long as people can recalibrate. Is that of understanding?

29. Hello ABE. We wish to clarify by asking our first question again - can you explain 'who' is ABE?

We are glad to come forth and clarify and we see that we have but already described what we are, but maybe a deeper knowing is of essence here? You see, we have to be careful as to not explain our way into thinking that you and we are of any indifference at all, not at core. We are but your original state of being, it is just that you do so have conditions of a body which creates different vibratory interference in a way. For you see, we do not have a physical body and are not of a point of place only, but when in communication with you both. The reason we are to come forth as ABE is because we are but a focal point of constricted consciousness shortened to become, or seem to become, separate - but we are not. You are just being receptive to this conscious flow and in this it has taken form in a sense through yourselves. See it as a radio station in which you would like to listen to. You tune in to certain channel, but you see you have but no preference and it is allowing more to come forth. Like we say, ABE is just a shortened constriction, of the whole thing - an abbreviation of pure consciousness. Is this of understanding now?

30. Is there anything ABE would wish to say to 'finalize' this book material - perhaps as an end message to the reader?

We would like to say that we are grateful for this communication and that there is always space and time, we are not in a great hurry. But we do so feel that this information is of importance now. People are the key connection, are the source, and unification is really what you are. You see, for something to become anything it starts with nothing; when all is seen that this is but the cycle of life then you could probably loosen up a little and allow all that you are to flow through you, unrestricted by what you have been conditioned to think, to be. The time is now to understand your extraordinary existence and at the same time your very ordinary existence - this is true unification of being. And you will see that you start to breathe again, you start to live again, and you start to love again. What a journey. You see, in this you realize you have come but full circle - but this time you are awake, you are alive. With much Love and Light - ABE.

Beautiful Traitor Books was founded in 2012 as an independent print-on-demand imprint to provide unusual and inspiring books for the discerning reader.

Our books are works that delve into various domains whether it is books for children, science fiction, social affairs, philosophy, theatre plays, or poetry. We have books translated into Spanish, French, Portuguese, Italian, and Hungarian.

All the books we publish seek to explore innovative and creative ideas. Many of them also tell a good story - stories that have different perspectives on life and on the human condition.

Beautiful Traitor Books is not only about offering the reader entertainment. We also seek to offer something that is like a nutrition; something of value that the reader can take away from the book. Good books function on more than one level. Put simply, we thrive on books that have the capacity to *shift* the reader.

Come and join the conversation – find out more at:

www.beautifultraitorbooks.com